SOARING SPIRIT

THIRTY-FIVE YEARS OF THE FORD THUNDERBIRD

SOARING SPIRIT

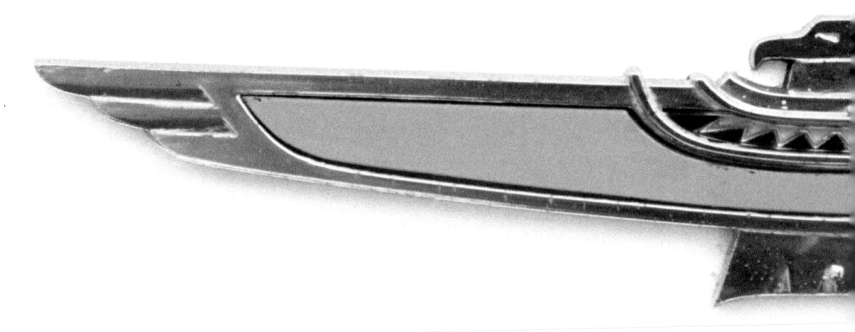

THIRTY-FIVE YEARS OF THE FORD THUNDERBIRD

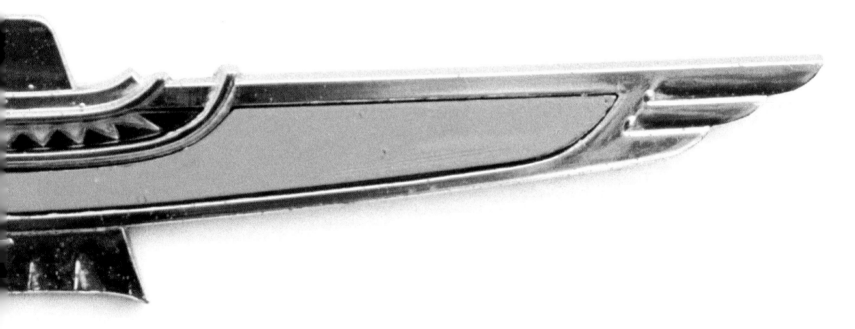

BY JOHN F. KATZ

PRODUCED BY THE STAFF OF AUTOMOBILE QUARTERLY

AUTOMOBILE QUARTERLY PUBLICATIONS

Editor for this Book: Julie Fenster
Book Design: Michael Pardo
Copy Editor: Chriss Bonhall

BOOK DIVISION

Charley Lloyd   Julie Fenster

MAGAZINE

President: Glenn F. Johns
Executive Editor: John F. Katz
Senior Editor: Jonathan A. Stein
Associate Editor: Bruce Feldman
European Editor: Griffith Borgeson
Art Director: Michael Pardo
Editorial Assistant: Letha Howard
Chief Photographer: Roy D. Query
Librarian: Tim Blank

AUTOMOBILE QUARTERLY, INC.
A Subsidiary of
The Kutztown Publishing Company, Inc.
Stephen J. Esser, President

Typesetting by Kutztown Publishing Company, Inc.,
Kutztown, Pennsylvania

Printing and binding by Ringier America,
New York, New York

Color Separations by Red Rose Graphics, Ltd.,
Lancaster, Pennsylvania

ISBN 0-915038-67-6: Automobile Quarterly, Inc.
Library of Congress Catalog Number: 89-081296

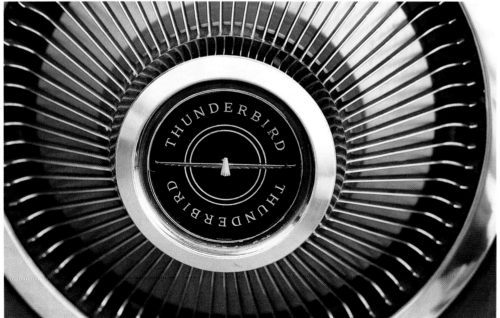

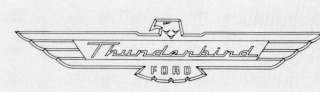

CONTENTS

INTRODUCTION

THUNDERBIRD. Hurtling down from the sky, hurling bolts of lightning from its talons as easily as a man might shoot an arrow. The Pawnees and other Native Americans of the Great Plains feared the Thunderbird, yet they painted its image on their drums and carved it in their ceremonial masks.

Thunderbird. The Kwakiutl of the rainy Northwest erected great totem poles to their ancestors. Many claimed the Thunderbird as their progenitor. They believed that each *namina*, or extended tribal family, had descended from a single supernatural spirit who had come down from heaven and taken human form. For this spirit alone was the top of the totem reserved.

Thunderbird. Descending from Dearborn, Michigan, in October 1954, it took the form of a two-seat *boulevardier*. The offspring of that original Thunderbird have been as varied as those in any human family: Some were distinguished, some were not; some hurled lightning bolts at the competition while others merely held their ground. All of them perched on top of Ford's product-line totem and from that vaunted position, each generation of the Thunderbird has reflected Ford's corporate self-image as much as it has represented the marketing strategies of its age.

In time, the Thunderbird would come to mirror the egos and aspirations of a few individuals at the top of Ford's organizational chart. But it was conceived in the Ford Division design studio in the summer of 1952, when the company was just emerging from the disaster that had been the Forties. . . .

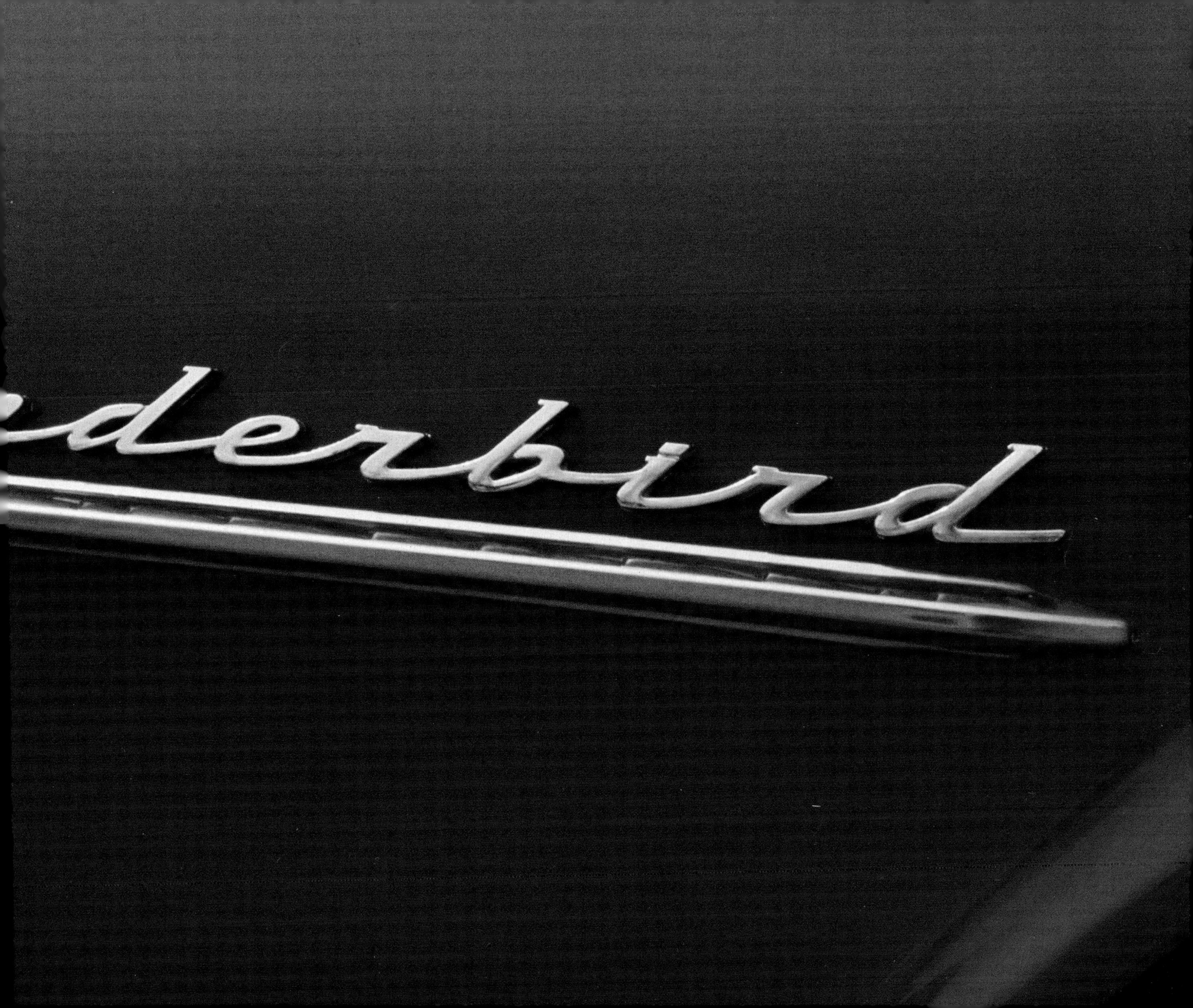
derbird

1

THUNDERBIRD TIME

1955-57

HENRY FORD, a brilliant, innovative visionary in his prime, grew stubborn and intractable in his old age. The premature death of his only son, Edsel, in 1943 had left the Ford Motor Company in a shambles; lacking leadership, it was losing close to $10 million a month by 1946. Control of the company fell to the eldest of Edsel's three sons, Henry Ford II, who was summoned home from the navy during World War II. After the war, he purged the company's entrenched, paranoid, and poorly-organized management, and effected a dramatic recovery. By the early Fifties, however, long before the reorganization was complete, production quotas and material shortages brought on by the Korean War threatened Ford's hard-won profitability.

The man at the top of the Ford Division totem then was Lewis D. Crusoe, a savvy financial manager who had been recruited from Bendix Aviation Corporation, along with the new executive vice president of Ford Motor Company, Ernest R. Breech. In Volume 9, Number 1 of *Automobile Quarterly*, author Karl Ludvigsen related how Crusoe visited the Paris Auto Salon in October 1951 with design consultant George Walker. Entranced by the Bugattis, Pegasos and Jaguars on display, Crusoe asked Walker why Ford couldn't build something similar. Walker recognized the voice of authority when he heard it and availed himself of the first opportunity to surreptitiously phone Dearborn and order his crew to have a sports-car project under way by the time Crusoe returned. Thus, the Thunderbird was born. . . .

> Philosophies changed . . . throughout Thunderbird history because of management. Everybody, whether it was Knudsen, or Iacocca, or Mr. Ford, or whomever, always singled out Thunderbird as their car to get involved in. It's the kind of car they like. They like to drive it, [and it's] the Ford Division's hot car, so they take a personal interest in overseeing its development. So . . . every president and every new vice-president of Ford Division that came along [had] a new philosophy on what the 'Bird ought to be and who they ought to sell it to, what the market share ought to be, and so forth."
>
> —Gale Halderman,
> director of Large and
> Luxury Exteriors,
> Ford Motor Company

. . . It's a wonderful tale, subtly suggesting all manner of romance and intrigue. But Franklin Q. Hershey insists that it just isn't true.

A professional designer since age 21, Hershey had honed his skills in the early Thirties, sketching custom Mercedes, Minervas, Cords and Duesenbergs for coachbuilder Walter M. Murphy of Pasadena, California. He then spent 20 high-pressure years with Harley Earl's pioneering Art and Colour Section at General Motors. Hershey embarked on his own metal-finishing business in Santa Fe, New Mexico, before joining Ford Division as Design Director in early 1952.

If Walker already had a sports car in the works, Hershey didn't know anything about it.

"The idea was mine in the first place," he asserted in April 1989. He had learned about the impending Corvette from a friend at GM and knew that Ford would need a response. Sometime during the summer of 1952, when the '55 Ford full-size line was safely completed, Hershey set aside a previously unused area in the styling studio and ordered a wooden armature on which a clay model could be built. With Studio Director Damon Woods, Hershey outlined the car's dimensions, at first with full-size drawings on a blackboard, then later on paper. The '56 face-lift for the full-size Fords, along with numerous truck and tractor projects, demanded Hershey's official time, so he assigned William P. Boyer "to keep things rolling" in the nascent sports-car department.

Boyer was then a "body development" designer at Ford, having been recruited from GM by Hershey the previous March. In his own book on the subject, *Thunderbird: An Odyssey in Automotive Design,*

Henry Ford II took control of the family business at age 25.

Designer Frank Hershey (right) fathered the sports car program that became the Thunderbird.

Consultant George Walker became Ford vice president, Design, in May 1955.

Boyer disputes Ludvigsen's account of Walker's quick action in Paris as the birth of the 'Bird. Former *AQ* Senior Editor Richard Langworth maintains that Ford's own archives contain no record of a sports-car project before Hershey started one in 1952. If Walker did indeed initiate a similar program a year before, it must have vanished, leaving no photos, no sketches, no trace.

Crusoe had, however, commissioned a market research study of the sports-car concept late in 1952, looking closely at Jaguar and MG buyers, as they had collectively accounted for about 12,000 new-car sales that year. Two of his findings in particular must have shaped the destiny of the Thunderbird. First, while many sports-car owners belonged to sports-car clubs, few actually raced their cars. Second, while Jaguar owners professed a high level of loyalty to their chosen marque, MG owners generally expressed a desire to trade up as soon as they were able. The researchers concluded that there was a market opportunity for a car priced between the MG and the Jaguar—say $3,000 to $3,500—but designed to be closer to the Jaguar in size, performance, and prestige.

In the months that followed, Ford management debated the wisdom of entering such a potentially volatile market. Hershey, knowing nothing about this, continued his own sports-car project in relative secrecy. This wasn't as difficult as it might sound; the Ford Division studio reported directly to Engineering and had only four full-time designers in its employ at that time. They brought a chassis engineer into their confidence to supply some realistic dimensions. (In his book, *The Thunderbird Story: Personal Luxury,* Richard Langworth reported that this was Ford Division Chief Engineer Bill Burnett. Hershey now contends that it was not Burnett but rather someone who worked for him. He couldn't recall the name.) Inevitably, perhaps, corporate Chief Engineer Earle S. MacPherson found out about Hershey's unauthorized project and threatened to end it.

"Ford Division was very skeptical," Hershey recalled. But by then it was late 1952, and the debate was about to be decided outside of Dearborn's halls. General Motors introduced the Corvette in January 1953. On February 9, Ford's corporate management approved Hershey's project, the project that would become the Thunderbird.

Woods and Boyer were by then nearly finished with their full-size clay model. Perhaps because Hershey's directives had been so clear, they had already arrived at what would be the definitive Thunderbird shape. As was common then (and now), the two sides of the model represented two slightly different styling concepts. The left side strongly resembled the upcoming Continental Mark II, with a strong rear-fender kickup that started just ahead of the door handle. The right side, though, *was* the definitive Thunderbird, save for a heavily chromed and tunneled taillight, resembling a jet-turbine exhaust. Joe Oros, a designer on Walker's staff, contributed the character line that ran forward from the taillight.

By March, the designers had shucked off the more exotic taillights, in favor of the plain, round units from the standard '55 Ford sedan. Ludvigsen said they were ordered to do this to keep costs down; Oros

agrees, but Langworth wrote that the goal was to maintain product identity. Hershey, though, claimed that the designers *wanted* the standard Ford taillights for their simplicity and that the heavily chromed monstrosities had been suggested by management.

Inevitably, some real compromises were made. The body engineers demanded that the bumper be moved below the grille. The specified power plant had a slightly higher-than-standard intake manifold with a carburetor spacer for better breathing, just when the stylists were trying to get the hood and cowl as low as possible. Boyer credited his colleague Dave Ash with the "power dome" solution, a functional hood scoop that cleared the air cleaner and became a T-Bird trademark. "Achieving a 36-inch-high cowl was like finding the Holy Grail," he added.

To streamline the engineering process, Chief Engineer Burnett cut up a '53 Ford sedan like a jigsaw puzzle and welded it back together as a proto-Thunderbird, on a 102-inch wheelbase, with the engine lowered and tucked back well behind the front wheels. This unlikely rig, dubbed the "Burnetti" by staffers, served as a test mule to evaluate the handling and braking characteristics of a vehicle with such novel weight distribution (novel in Detroit, at least).

Ultimately the engineers gave the Thunderbird a unique box-section frame with an X-braced center. Most of the 'Bird's running gear,

however, was gathered from the parts shelves. Fortunately, Ford had adopted a double-wishbone independent suspension for all its products in '49, adapting it to balljoints for Lincoln in 1952 and for the rest of the corporate lineup in 1954. (Balljoints, in fact, were originally devised by MacPherson as necessary adduces to the suspension formula that would make him immortal.) Ford engineers added rubber bump stops to limit acceleration windup of the Thunderbird's Hotchkiss rear end. The original steering gear required only 3.5 turns lock-to-lock—fast then, and quite reasonable by modern standards—and the Thunderbird was the first American car to boast tubeless tires as standard equipment.

Naturally, Ford engineers chose their brand-new (for 1954) ohv V-8 to power their new roadster. Although early press releases said the car would be packing the 256-cubic-inch Mercury edition of the new engine, Ford ultimately increased that engine's stroke by .125-inch and its bore by .200-inch, boosting total displacement to 292 cubic inches. A compression ratio of 8.1:1 yielded 190 bhp in manual-shift cars; automatics, with 8.5:1 compression, produced 198. A manual lockout prevented the automatic transmission gear selector from being shifted through Neutral without depressing a button on the top of the lever—a Thunderbird innovation that has since been adopted by the industry worldwide.

Ford officially established a marketing department for what would become the Thunderbird in late summer of 1953, with Thomas B. Case as product manager. In late September 1953, just after the Paris Auto Salon, Crusoe dropped the green flag for production—more than a year after Hershey had started his secret sports-car project. In November, Crusoe decided to debut a prototype at the Detroit Auto Show in February 1954.

Actually, the car that would appear at the show was a wooden mockup and some of its details (wheel covers, for example, and headlight bezels) still weren't final. More important, it needed a name.

Ford's advertising agency, J. Walter Thompson, rounded up a list of candidates, including inspirations such as Fordette, Fordster, Beaver, Detroiter, Hep Cat, Flag Liner, and Wheelaway. Crusoe offered a $250 suit of clothes to anyone who could do better. (Boyer noted that, in Detroit in 1954, no store even *sold* a suit that cost as much as $250 . . . but then, Crusoe's own favorite contender in the name game was Savile, suggesting that he appreciated an expensive new suit as much as anyone.) Stylist Alden R. "Gib" Giberson finally suggested the name Thunderbird. This appealed to Southwest-raised Hershey and, more important, Crusoe liked it, as well. Giberson, himself a Southwesterner, later created the original silver-and-turquoise Thunderbird emblem.

In August 1954, with the Thunderbird design basically finished and the first brochures printed, Hershey left for a brief vacation. This was the first time that Walker went to see the prototype Thunderbird. He suggested that, for product identity, the T-Bird carry the same broad, V-shaped molding on its side as the '55 Fairlane: a sort of huge, chrome check-mark that divided two-tone paint schemes on the big sedan. By the time Hershey returned, Crusoe had ordered the brochures changed and the styling studios had built prototypes with two slightly different versions of the check-mark trim. "I blew my stack," said Hershey, who promptly gathered MacPherson as an ally and took his case directly to Henry Ford II. Ford reluctantly vetoed Walker's idea, but Crusoe salvaged a prototype pair of the trim pieces for his personal T-Bird.

Boyer credited Chief Body Engineer Henry Grebe with maintaining the "integrity of the car," and with saving it from the compromises that afflicted the early Corvette. The Thunderbird, Hershey confirmed, was intended from the beginning to one-up the 'Vette, not compete directly against it. He said it was Ford Product Planning Chief Chase Morsey who coined the term "personal car." The Thunderbird was to be, as Hershey described it, "a car that a bank president or corporate head could drive without making a lot of noise and having people point and say, 'Look who still thinks he's a kid.' " Thus, when the 'Bird debuted on October 22, 1954, its $2,695 base price included roll-up side windows, an adjustable steering column and six-way power seats. Ford's press relations crew vehemently denied that it was a sports car, in any way suitable for competition.

The first full tests were only a few months away. *Motor Trend* editor Walt Woron loudly proclaimed in December 1954 that "although the

This page: Engineer Bill Burnett cobbled together the "Burnetti" prototype (top left) from pieces of a '53 Ford sedan. To lower its center of gravity, he later discarded the body entirely in favor of one from a fiberglass kit car. Ford Division General Manager Lewis Crusoe (left, in light suit) discusses the T-Bird with Henry Ford II.

These pages and page 9: 1955 Thunderbird, owned by George Watts. Bearing serial number P5FH-100005, it is acknowledged as the first production Thunderbird. (Cars 100001-100004 were full-size Fords.) Only the earliest '55s were fitted with chrome-trimmed, Fairlane-style headlight bezels and plain fender skirts. Most '55 'Birds had plain headlight bezels and chrome gravel shields on the fender skirts—just like the '56 models.

The Thunderbird is now available in 5 colors!

6 a.m. THUNDERBIRD time

Doctor, Lawyer, Merchant, Chief—no matter who you are—you'll find yourself getting up early when your garage is home to a Thunderbird. For here is a truly delightful package of sheer pleasure—all the way from its "let's go" look to the "let's go" performance of its Thunderbird Special Y-block V-8.

What's more—that seat is nearly *five feet* wide and it's power-operated. A touch of a switch moves it *up, down—* forward or back to suit your requirements for driving comfort. The steering wheel is another comfort feature—adjust it as *you* like it.

As for weather—your Thunderbird can have an easily demountable hard top *and* or a snug fabric top that folds away completely out of sight. Windows roll up . . . power-operated if you like. Power steering, power brakes, Overdrive and Speed-Trigger Fordomatic are also available. These are important details, but the main thing is the low and mighty car itself! Why don't you obey that urge and try one today? Your Ford Dealer is the man to see.

This is the Thunderbird Special Y-block V-8 4-barrel carburetor, 8.5 to 1 compression ratio, 198-h.p. with Fordomatic . . . try it!

An exciting original by **FORD**

001 BRD   CALIFORNIA

Ford Motor Co. is the first one to deny it, they have a *sports car* in the Thunderbird, and it's a good one. . . . The more I drove it, the more I liked it,'' gushed Woron, praising the T-Bird's dashboard layout, as well as its straight-line performance. He noted that the automatic's eight extra horsepower kept it dead even in the drags with the stick-shift model, reaching 60 mph from a standing start in 11 seconds flat. But what Woron really liked was the way the Thunderbird handled: confidently, with no surprises, just as the engineers intended. "You can take any given curve," wrote Woron, "at 10-15 mph more than [in] the [full-size] '55 Ford." About the only thing Woron could find to complain about was a closed-in feeling when the hardtop, with its blind quarters, was in place.

With celebrated club racer Jack McAfee at the wheel in March 1955, *Road & Track* lowered Woron's 0 to 60 time to 9.5 seconds and coaxed the 'Bird through the quarter-mile in just 16.9 seconds, but recorded a somewhat disappointing top speed of 110.1 actual mph (125 indicated) for an automatic model with the 3.31:1 axle. The Thunderbird also disappointed *R&T* with its ever-present understeer. However, being impressed with the 'Bird's high-speed stability and "really excellent riding qualities," the *R&T* purists allowed that it could be rightly called "a touring-sports car, designed to give sports-car qualities up to a point, combined with enough comfort to satisfy the most delicate of constitutions. It is an extremely practical machine for personal transport over any distance in any kind of weather."

The two hallmark changes for 1956—the external spare tire and porthole quarter window—were purely children of necessity. Crusoe himself had complained of poor rearward visibility with the top in place. The obvious solution was to build conventional quarter windows into the top. These proved costly and difficult to seal, yet they were still approved for 1956 production as late as May 1955, when someone decided that they didn't look all that good. A more imaginative solution was on the horizon. Recalling the formal coachwork of another era, the designers quickly suggested the now-famous circular window. Just in case the round window struck anyone as peculiar however, the blind-quarter tops were offered as a no-cost option through 1957. The porthole tops outsold them, four to one.

Crusoe also complained of inadequate ventilation, a problem that was solved by the pop-out cowl vents found on '56-57 Thunderbirds. Oh, and one more thing, he said: The car needed a back seat—as if adding such an amenity wouldn't transform the Thunderbird into a completely different automobile.

The back seat, of course, would come in '58; in the meantime, the 'Bird would merely have a bigger trunk. The product planners had quickly realized that the T-Bird would never be the darling of the country-club set if it didn't have a place in which to park at least one set of golf clubs. The popular Continental kit of Fifties fame offered a quick-and-dirty solution: Getting the spare out of the trunk left more room for woods, mashies and niblicks. Ford dealers were already handling one aftermarket atrocity that provided a rear-mounted spare tire, but also stretched the bumper and exhaust tips about 12 inches rearward. "It just wasn't acceptable on a piece of sporting machinery," wrote Boyer. The factory solution was to wrap a heavy-duty bumper bar around the external spare, intersecting it with thin, blade-like half-bumpers on either side. While they were at it, the stylists tidied things up by relocating the exhaust tips to the outer corners of the bumper—where, not coincidentally, they would appear on the '56 Fairlane. Even though this result looked far more graceful than any aftermarket kit, the design was not released for production until an incredibly late July 1955.

The outboard spare caused some practical problems, such as an unacceptable amount of shake and flex in a frame that was never designed to carry it. By the time Burnett's engineers were through shoring up the structure, the '56 'Bird weighed about 350 pounds more than the '55 model—and most of that was hanging out behind the rear wheels. Responding to consumer complaints, Burnett had already specified longer, *softer* rear springs to transfer some of the car's roll stiffness to the front end. Now fearing oversteer from the heavy tail, Burnett dictated a drastic, last-minute reduction in the steering ratio.

Modern Thunderbird collectors contend, surprisingly, that all this diddling brought a net improvement in handling. *Road & Track* felt otherwise, noting in its August 1956 issue that the changes had switched the T-Bird's weight distribution from 52/48 to 49/51. The softer springs allowed an alarming amount of squat on acceleration, and the testers judged the T-Bird's overall handling to be "fair to good in comparison to domestic sedans, but abominable for a 2-seater machine." At least the new, optional, 312-cubic-inch, 225bhp V-8 allowed the 3570-pound 'Bird to beat its lighter predecessor to 60 mph by 0.2 second and to give up only 0.1 second on the way to the quarter.

Of course, 1956 was the year that the Thunderbird's fiberglass rival, the Corvette, acquired roll-up windows (with optional power assist), an optional hardtop, and external door handles. It was also the year that *Motor Trend* did the inevitable: Walt Woron clamped his fifth wheel on both contenders and let the chips fall.

The two cars were remarkably alike in price: $3,145 for the 'Vette as tested, $3,148 for the 'Bird. Not surprisingly, the Corvette outpaced the T-Bird down the straights and around the curves. But the 'Bird rode better. *MT's* astonishing conclusion? "The Corvette. . .feels more like a sports car." The Thunderbird, Woron noted, was already losing ground to big sedans that were improving every year in handling.

Curiously, the British press proved more appreciative of the Thunderbird's virtues. While allowing that "the suspension—and handling as a whole—is not up to the highest standards of European *gran tourismo* machinery," *The Autocar* for February 10, 1956, positively raved about the T-Bird's ability to maintain a stable and comfortable 90-to-100-mph cruising speed over "the indifferently surfaced roads of France." Most European sports cars just didn't have that kind of speed. Not that any of this probably mattered back in Dearborn. Ford had sold 16,155 Thunderbirds in 1955 and would sell 15,631 more in '56. Chevrolet wouldn't move nearly that many Corvettes out the door until the advent of the Sting Ray in 1963.

Crusoe was named executive vice president of Car and Truck Groups in January 1955. The new divisional general manager was Robert McNamara, formerly with the Army's Department of Logistics. He was one of the "Whiz Kids," who stormed into the business after the war. McNamara was a bottom-line man, perhaps even more so than Crusoe. "He really wasn't much of a car man," recalled Hershey in a perfect understatement quoted in the September 1985 issue of *Car Collector*. On December 30, 1954, Crusoe and McNamara met to discuss the Ford Division's product-line future. The Thunderbird, they said, was "not to be referred to as 'the sports car.'" It needed a bigger trunk, independent rear suspension and fuel injection for 1957. For 1958, it should get a back seat and a station wagon option.

Hershey had put Rhys Miller in charge of the 1956 and '57 facelifts late in 1954. At that point, no one in the Ford studio was seriously thinking about a four-seater (that decision was made official on March 9, 1955), but one of the design criteria set out for the continuing two-seater was that there had to be room for both a golf bag *and* a spare tire in the trunk. Miller lengthened the T-bird's tail just enough to accommodate the required gear, and the net result was still four inches shorter than the '56 with its external spare. The McNamara/Crusoe summit specified bright, aluminum-lined coves behind the front wheel openings, but these were mercifully abandoned when the '56 Corvette appeared in August 1955.

Ludvigsen, writing in *Sports Cars Illustrated* for January 1957, noted that the relocated spare, combined with stiffer rear springs, provided a generally better ride with less pitching. However, resolute understeer had returned as the T-Bird's dominant handling characteristic. With 9.7:1 compression, the 312 cid engine now produced 245 bhp—enough, according to the May 1957 issue of *Speed Age,* to hustle the 'Bird to 60 mph in a hair under 8.5 seconds.

With a few exceptions, the Thunderbird's forays into road racing were unmitigated disasters; its performance was limited as much by brake fade as by indifferent handling. Similarly, serious aerodynamic lift limited its stability on NASCAR ovals. But the Thunderbird succeeded in trouncing its competition at the Daytona Speed Weeks. In 1955, a 'Bird sponsored by Tom McCahill and driven by Joe Ferguson was clocked at 124.633 mph, bettered in its class only by a Jaguar XK-120M. In '56, legendary racer and tuning wizard Peter De Paolo prepared a Speed Week Thunderbird for Heinzelman Ford of Daytona, Florida, taking advantage of the 230bhp/dual-4bbl setup offered that year as an option. Driven by Chuck Daigh in the Production Sports Car class, De Paolo's 'Bird won the standing-mile honors at 88.779 mph. Another 'Bird thundered into second at 87.889 mph, comfortably ahead of John Fitch's third-place Corvette at 86.872 mph. Even the Corvette's chief engineer, Zora Arkus-Duntov, managed only 89.735 mph in the Modified class.

The independent rear suspension never materialized for '57, nor did fuel injection. De Paolo suggested a McCulloch centrifugal supercharger instead. With a single 4bbl carburetor and 8.5:1 compression,

Opposite and above: 1956 Thunderbird, owned by F.W. Krekel

Robert McNamara, who succeeded Crusoe as Ford Division general manager, demanded a bigger, four-passenger Thunderbird for '58.

1957 Thunderbird, owned by Robert H. Walker. With serial number F7FH381487, this is one of 194 supercharged, 300bhp "F-Birds."

16

Ford conservatively rated the force-fed 312 cid V-8 at 300 bhp. Known as "F-Birds" because of their special serial number prefix, only 194 such supercharged T-Birds were built, most with automatic transmissions. Langworth claimed to have personally clocked one from 0 to 60 mph in 5.5 seconds, admittedly without correction for speedometer error. Ford built 14 more supercharged 'Birds with manual transmissions and a D prefix, strictly for NASCAR homologation. Daigh and De Paolo returned to Daytona with just such a D-Bird and scored 93.312 mph in the Production Sports Car standing-start mile, only to be kept from the flying mile by engine failure.

As Langworth has pointed out, the two-seat Thunderbird may not have been a sports car, but it certainly was a *performance* car. Its styling broke no new ground, yet its clean lines and near-perfect proportions have remained a part of our consciousness. As a quintessential American icon, the two-seat Thunderbird still flashes, forever young, through rock videos and popular films. Its image lingered in the Sixties as well, even as its descendants grew bloated and prosaic, awaiting the Eighties' performance renaissance.

McNamara wanted bright metal fender coves for the T-Bird's '57 facelift (above) until a similar treatment appeared on the '56 Corvette. Note the potential competitors parked in the background in this Ford Design photo: Studebaker President Speedster, Triumph TR-2 or TR-3, Chevrolet Corvette, MG TF. Screen idol Clark Gable (left) had a two-speed McCulloch supercharger fitted to his '56.

2

FLIGHT PLAN CLEARED

1958-66

FRANK HERSHEY disliked the '58 Thunderbird instantly—probably for the same reasons that Gale Halderman remembers it fondly . . . Halderman, who now heads Ford's Large and Luxury Car studio, joined the company in 1954, when the '55 two-seat Thunderbird was already a reality. The first Thunderbird he worked on was the '58 four-seater. And, as excessive as that particular exercise may appear today, it was fairly restrained by the standards of the late Fifties. As Halderman put it, "It all kind of seemed clear at the time," and his eyes sparkled with the reminiscence.

Yes, Gale Halderman recalled the '58 fondly and perhaps rightly so; with its vanguard unitized construction, the so-called "Square-bird" was far more advanced, technologically, than its two-seat ancestor. Body Engineer Bob Hennessy had achieved the seemingly impossible, providing interior room and comfort equivalent to Ford's full-size sedans in a car that sat a full 10 inches lower. The '58 T-Bird's final height of 52.5 inches, in fact, was only about an inch taller than the two-seater with its hardtop in place.

Nonetheless, clay development of a two-seater for 1958 continued as late as February '57. No one had defended the little car more staunchly than Hershey himself, who had taken his case to McNamara as the sales results rolled in. Hershey pointed out that the two-seater could continue at its 1955 volume using existing dies that were already paid for. After all, Ford had sold more than 16,000 two-seaters in '55—60 percent more than what had originally been projected. But

> "[It was] very sculptured. Had a bomb on the side that flowed back into the bumper system. It had a lot of action going on. . . . I think the goal we had was to make the car distinctive—almost to the point where it was controversial."
>
> —Gale Halderman

McNamara said that that just wasn't enough.

Product Manager Thomas Case actually phoned the Budd Company, which built the two-seater bodies, in September 1957 to ask what it would cost to keep the original 'Bird in production. Within 30 minutes, McNamara summoned Case and scolded him. "It's dead," he said of the two-seater, "I don't ever want to hear of it again."

The survival of the two-seater would not have been as simple as a continuing contract with the Budd Company, anyway. Ford's great River Rouge plant in Detroit, where the two-seat Thunderbirds were assembled side-by-side with Customs and Fairlanes and the like, was seriously overcrowded, particularly on the trim line. Additionally, Ford's full-size cars had been largely redesigned for '57 and many components that were shared in '55 and '56 were by 1957 unique to the Thunderbird—making it harder to justify continued production of the low-volume model.

The high resale value of the two-seaters cast some doubt on the matter, yet surveys conducted by both Ford and *Popular Mechanics* found that about 30 percent of two-seater owners thought that a back seat would be an improvement. Product Planning had developed a worst-case scenario in which the four-seater sold no better than the two-seater, resulting in a $3-million to $7-million loss over a three-year period. To McNamara's credit, he defended the 'Bird against corporate conservatives who felt even the four-seater was an unnecessary risk. It was also his effort that kept the Thunderbird in the Ford ranks, fending off efforts by Lincoln-Mercury to snatch the car away, now that it was becoming more luxury-oriented.

In any case, McNamara had guessed right about the marketability of a four-seater. Despite a late start (production didn't begin until January, with convertibles following in June), Ford sold 37,892 four-seaters during the 1958 model year. That number would rise to 67,456 in '59 and to 92,843 in 1960. The latter figure would stand for 16 years as the high point for Thunderbird sales.

By 1957, Ford was able to lower its full-size, separate-frame models about 5.3 inches by curving the frame side rails out around the edges of the passenger compartment. But the unit-body Thunderbird sat lower still. Comparing the dimensions of the '58 Thunderbird to the full-size Fairlane of the same year is quite revealing:

	1958 Thunderbird (inches)	1958 Fairlane (inches)
Wheelbase	113.0	118.0
Length	205.4	207.2
Width	77.0	78.0
Height	52.5	56.2
Ground Clearance	5.8	6.0
Front Legroom	43.4	43.2
Front Headroom	34.5	33.8
Rear Legroom	38.8	40.8
Rear Headroom	33.3	33.6

Henry Grebe, then director of Body Engineering, spearheaded the shift to unitized construction (in which a very rigid body requires no separate frame) primarily to save weight. Many of Ford's decision-makers had by then deduced that it would be the wave of the future. Ford even constructed a new assembly plant at Wixom, Michigan, specifically for building unit-body vehicles. The '58 Lincolns would be built there as well; the Marketing Department hoped that unitized construction would endow Ford's then-languishing luxury line with a new, high-technology image.

Henry Ford appointed George Walker vice-president, Design, in May 1955. Hershey, wary because of previous conflicts with Walker, resigned the same day. Walker appointed Joe Oros as chief stylist of the Ford Studios in March 1956, and Oros made Boyer manager of the Thunderbird studio.

The styling theme of the first four-seat Thunderbird, especially the "dual pod" configuration of the rear, was developed originally as a major '58 face-lift of the two-seat original. "The '58 was also influenced by the 1957 Ford car-wide front fender," Oros said. "With dual headlights, low hood, into a contemporary mouth bumper grille." But the four-seater's low roofline and unitized construction left its passengers sitting in a deep channel between the high driveline tunnel and the high doorsills that were necessary to give the body stiffness. After some contemplation, Boyer decided that he could make a virtue of this vice. "We couldn't get rid of the tunnel," he wrote, "so the most obvious solution was to make the tunnel a feature." Taking a

Preceding page: 1958 Thunderbird hardtop, owned by Dr. Lloyd A. Budwig. These pages: "Squarebird" rear-end theme first appeared in the summer of '55 as a proposal for a '58 two-seater (left). Another '58 two-seater concept from the same period predicted the headrest fairings of the '62 Sports Roadster (opposite), while clay four-door (below) presaged '64 Mustang grille opening and side scoop.

21

1959 Thunderbird convertible (above), owned by Gordon G. Allen; 1960 Thunderbird hardtop (opposite), equipped with rare sunroof option, owned by Del & Julie Battista. Note chrome air deflector atop its windshield.

cue from the aircraft industry, his designers fashioned a sleek, handsome, full-length center console between the bucket seats. As obvious as this seems today, it was then a new idea, and of course it set a precedent that personal cars still follow three decades later.

The console bisected the interior of the car, an effect the designers decided to emphasize by dividing the dashboard into two large, symmetrical pods, with a flat area in between. This, of course, blended perfectly with the split-down-the-middle look that had already been proposed for the rear end of the '58 roadster. According to Boyer:

> This theme would carry through the back light into the rear bucket seat backs and coordinate with the dual cowl instrument

Ford considered several radical face-lifts for the '60 'Bird, including this rather unabashed turbojet theme (right). Ultimately, though, only grille, taillight and trim changes distinguished production '60s from their '58-59 counterparts.

panel straddling the high tunnel. [It] would look great in the top-down configuration, and the tunnel leading into the crash pad, with its double-cockpit look, was quite exciting and new.

At Oros' request, Boyer adapted the familiar shape of the two-seater's hardtop into an upright and formal roofline; this enhanced rear-seat headroom, as well as ease of entry/exit, while allowing the rear deck to remain fashionably low and long. The shape of the roof, said Halderman, was deliberately out-of-step with the times: "It was quite a shock, frankly, to see it. You had to take a second look at it. [But] it became so popular, they put it on the [full-size] two-door Ford a few years later . . ."

And, of course, it started the Thunderbird tradition of a formal roof, which, in Halderman's words, "has lingered on for a long time."

To further assist adult passengers in climbing into the rear seat with some semblance of grace and dignity, Boyer's designers stretched the doors out to a hefty 48.74 inches (yes, more than four feet)—opening all the way back at the leading edge of the rear seat. This, in turn, required Body Engineering to develop a special door hinge to take the torsional load. The engineers also invested considerable time and money developing a convertible top that would flip backward into the trunk, keeping the rear deck absolutely clear (and the trunk almost useless). A cross-flow radiator helped keep the front end low, and all structural parts were galvanized to prevent rust. In all, Ford spent a then-staggering $40 million re-engineering the Thunderbird for '58.

Even at that, the T-Bird still shared most of its running gear with its humbler Ford brethren. That meant double A-arms and coil springs in front (Engineer MacPherson nearly succeeded in planting his struts there before financial considerations uprooted the idea), in addition to a live rear axle suspended on long, substantial trailing arms, with coil springs, a Panhard rod, and small anti-torque links. The only engine offered was a 352 cid V-8 that was rated at 300 bhp.

Sports Cars Illustrated for April 1958 praised the big 'Bird's impressive acceleration: 0 to 60 mph in 10.4 seconds and a standing quarter mile in 17.8. Cornering, the editors noted, was accompanied by a great deal of lean. However, with near 50/50 weight distribution, the 'Bird maintained a controllable, neutral attitude and gave plenty of warning before gentle but terminal oversteer took it off the road. Steering was described as light but too slow. In May, *Motor Trend* handed the T-Bird its Car of the Year Award for 1958, noting Ford's "totally new concept in interior packaging." The *MT* editors added that "the ride of the new Thunderbird is as comfortable as any American car today, regardless of size."

The '59 and '60 Thunderbirds were little changed, mostly because the '58 model had busted the development budget for the subsequent three years. It was probably just as well.

North American Design has retained photos of the various proposals that *weren't* built; most involve sportier but less distinctive rooflines, with jet-powered front- and rear-end treatments that would have done justice to the jukeboxes onboard Emperor Ming's battle cruisers.

Elwood Engel's proposal for the '61 Thunderbird (right and below right) actually spawned the '61 Continental. Photos indicate that Engel tried out several subtle variations on this same theme. Flamboyant alternative (bottom) appears to have originated the '64 T-Bird front fender.

The '58 Thunderbird's trailing-arm rear suspension had been designed primarily for easy conversion to an air-spring system, but the air springs just didn't hold up. (Ford installed air springs in 200 1958 full-size cars but not in any T-Birds.) So the design was scrapped for '59, in favor of two long semi-elliptic springs. On the plus side, the '59 'Bird got the 430-cid, 350-bhp Lincoln V-8 as an option, and the convertible top became fully automatic.

Road & Track, in its June 1959 issue, criticized the 'Bird's "sundry unrelated curves, bulges, and sharp edges" and complained of slow, numb steering and poor directional stability. Yet the editors clocked a satisfying 0 to 60-mph time of 8.2 seconds with the 430 V-8. One hundred mph, *R&T* noted, was attainable in only 24 seconds, with the quarter mile passing in 16.2.

Ironically, it was a '59 Thunderbird that scored the single most conspicuous racing success in the history of the breed. The inaugural event at the brand-new Daytona 2.5-mile tri-oval speedway was a 500-mile contest for NASCAR stock cars—which, in those days, truly were *stock* cars. Johnny Beauchamp's T-Bird chased Lee Petty's Oldsmobile all the way to a photo finish. Even though the officials gave the race to Petty, the Squarebird had proven that it could run with the best, in a way that its two-seat elders never had.

Back in Dearborn, sales of all Ford, Lincoln, Mercury and Edsel passenger cars totaled 1,647,184 for the 1959 model year, accounting for a full 27.7 percent of the U.S. market. Henry Ford II moved up to the chairman's office in 1960, and the board of directors selected McNamara to take his place as president. The new Ford Division general manager was a 35-year-old marketing man from Pennsylvania named Lido A. Iacocca. It is difficult to imagine a more exuberant design than that of the 1961 Thunderbird—or a guiding spirit who would shape the destiny of the car more than Lee Iacocca.

The '61 'Bird could have been quite different. The '55-'57 and '58-'60 Thunderbirds had more or less followed a single path from concept to completion. By late 1958, however, several competing studios were developing very distinct styling themes for 1961. Halderman still remembers the spirit of tight competition; everyone wanted to be the creator of "the next style."

This included staff stylist Elwood P. Engel, one of Walker's appointees, who supervised the L-M studio in the late Fifties. He had set aside a long basement room for his pet projects: It was so narrow that one long wall had to be mirrored to allow visitors to see both sides of the clay model in progress. The stylists who worked there (including John Najjar, Robert Thomas and Colin Neale) referred to it as "the stiletto room" or "submarine service."

In this underground hideaway, Engel sculpted *his* Thunderbird, a three-dimensional repudiation of the excess of the late Fifties. As Engel told author Dave Emanuel for an *Automobile Quarterly* article that appeared in 1985 (Volume 23, Number 4):

In those days, all the cars were pretty monstrous—the bumpers, grilles and ornamentation were God-awful. They just went too far. So . . . I made damn sure it didn't have any of those big, heavy-looking torpedo bumper guards or fins . . .

The model was European in concept and exceptionally handsome, with utterly clean, oh-so-subtle radiuses in the side sheetmetal and a tight, formal, close-coupled greenhouse (the upper portion of the car). Most characteristic was an understated razor-edge that ran uninterrupted, arrow-straight and level from the front end of the front fender to the neat, wraparound taillight at the rear. Engel told Langworth: "McNamara came down there one day and looked at it. . . He said, 'I wonder what this would be like if it was a Continental?' "

It took Engel only a few weeks to add 18 inches of wheelbase and a second set of doors. His favorite Thunderbird proposal entered production as the 1961 Lincoln Continental, almost exactly as he had designed it, down to its very un-torpedo-like bumper guards. The new look was so successful that Lincoln sales rose an encouraging 10.6 percent in the 1961 model year. In a way, the Thunderbird had surrendered its best design proposal to save the Lincoln. Twenty years later, Lincoln would repay the debt. . .

Engel's other studios had created different designs that shared the same slab sides, blade-like fender tops and short greenhouse. Meanwhile, Joe Oros had blasted off in the opposite direction. Under his direction, Boyer and Woods created a clean-lined, flamboyant rocket ship on wheels with a pointed prow and heavily skirted rear fenders. One Boyer proposal even featured abrupt, sharply rising tailfins that could have been borrowed from a Redstone rocket.

Walker openly supported the Engel theme for the Thunderbird. Oros remembers being summoned to the Rotunda by Henry Ford and asked, with Walker present, which one *he* favored. The gravity of the situation was not lost on Oros; he knew that, to defend his design, he would have to disagree with his boss—in front of Henry II.

"Mr. Ford," he replied, bravely indicating his own work, "I believe it should be this one. It's racy, purposeful, aerodynamic and more apropos to a sporty car."

Although Mr. Ford didn't say so then, he must have agreed.

The rocket shape (which Boyer described, alternately, as the "fuselage" or the "projectile" look) survived, but with more subtle fins integrated with a bumper-to-taillight razor edge reminiscent of Engel's proposals. (The fender ridges on both cars, said Oros, were suggested by Body Engineering to simplify the fender stampings.) The jet-exhaust taillights (Engel likened them to flowerpots), latent since 1955, found an appropriate home at the rear end of this creation. Like the grille and bumpers, they were beautifully integrated into the form of the car. "We could never do anything like that on the [full-size] Ford because of cost and weight," said Oros, referring to the acres of chrome bumper stock that surrounded the taillights and grille.

Like Hershey before him, however, Oros found out that a designer's vacation can be a dangerous undertaking. "Prior to its introduction," Oros recalled, "the dealers got hold of photographs. Some were quite concerned that they'd lose their shirts on the car. They thought the

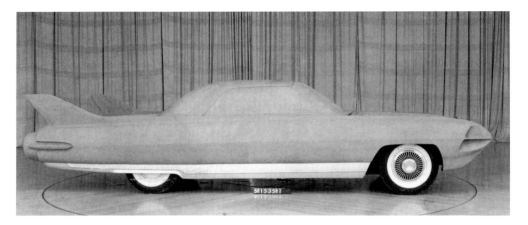

Cadillac-esque proposal with steep, rocket-like fins (above) was considered only briefly, but the "projectile" theme it established (left and below left) evolved into the production '61 'Bird.

Young Lee Iacocca backed Sports Roadster and triple-carb option.

1961 Thunderbird Hardtop, owned by Ronald A. Curtis. Note the slight "fender" ridges on top of the engine hood. Optional "Swing-Away" steering wheel pivoted 10 inches to the right to ease entry and exit.

car was too far out." Apparently, the way that the engine hood ran flat across the front of the car, with no clearly defined fender shapes, had the dealers alarmed. (Chevrolet had had a tough time unloading a similarly afflicted full-size car in 1959.) They took their case to Ford management only days before Oros had planned to leave for a well-earned vacation in Europe. Walker assigned Engel to make the necessary changes. Worried that the car's integrity would be violated in his absence, Oros almost turned back at the airport.

From Europe, he phoned Damon Woods at the studio every day. "It wasn't much of a vacation," he lamented. "But nothing worked out properly, because the whole car was so integrated. And tooling was so far along." Ultimately, the studio added only two subtle windsplits to the top of the hood, suggesting a conventional fender ridge. "When I came back from Europe," said Oros, "I was quite pleased to see that that was all that had happened." He succeeded in having the spurious ridges removed from the '62 model.

With the new look came new engineering. Although the wheelbase of the '61 'Bird remained 113 inches, and all other key body dimensions were within an inch of its predecessor's, the '61 unit body was in fact all-new and much improved, welded up in two rigid sections which were then joined at the cowl. The cowl structure itself was lowered to improve both styling and visibility and was sufficiently similar to the Continental's to simplify tooling at Wixom. For the same reason, the T-Bird and Lincoln shared a windshield and some other body parts.

The engineers also scrapped most of the old 'Bird's running gear. The front wheels were now located by narrow lower arms with drag struts, and the coil springs were relocated to the upper, wishbone-shape arms. This arrangement reduced ride harshness by allowing the front wheels to move *back*—as well as up—as they encountered bumps in the road. Mercedes-Benz had pioneered the principle a few years before, and Lincoln had adopted it previously. But the 1961 Ford Thunderbird, Mercury Meteor 800 and Mercury Monterey were the first cars to apply this geometry to the rear wheels as well, by mounting the forward ends of the semi-elliptic springs in thick rubber bushings. The new suspension provided an extra inch of track at the front and three more inches in the rear. At the same time, the engineers quickened the steering ratio (back to 3.5 turns lock-to-lock, like the original two-seater) and increased the brake lining area 14 percent.

The basic ohv V-8 reappeared for another season, now bored 0.05-inch wider and stroked 0.28-inch longer for a total displacement of 390 cubic inches. Despite the increase, Ford claimed the same 300 bhp as before, but peak torque rose significantly, from 381 lb-ft to 427. The 430 was no longer offered. Manual transmissions, never popular, were at last removed from the Thunderbird menu, and at the same time power assists for steering and brakes became standard.

"The glamour car of the Ford line," noted *Motor Trend* in May, "has been completely changed—for the better." The editors meant it; the next two pages were filled with a veritable litany of improvements, encompassing visibility, seating comfort, entry/exit, ride, braking and,

perhaps most significantly, handling: "Last year's Thunderbird had rather vague, sluggish handling, but not the new model. The '61 can be maneuvered with precision in almost any driving consideration." Directional stability, it seems, had been transformed overnight from abysmal to "excellent," body sway was "sharply reduced" and steering made "nimbler." Too little damping, though, still allowed "wild float at highway speeds." The 4,110-pound 'Bird attained 60 mph in a "not spectacular" 10.5 seconds. But aside from some minor ergonomic mistakes and the still-useless trunk of the convertible, the *MT* testers found few faults as they nearly fell over one another listing the Thunderbird's new-found virtues.

Nineteen sixty-two brought mild but welcome styling refinements: a new grille texture that turned down the flash somewhat, and more complementary chrome ornamentation on the side. It nearly brought front-wheel drive as well; Advanced Car and Engineering staffer Frederick J. Hooven had had such a proposal under development since 1958, hoping to sling the low-slung T-Bird even lower. His department spent $3 million developing a driveline before management de-

1962 Thunderbird Sports Roadster (opposite), owned by Lois C. Eminger. "Constellation" (top) and "Italienne" (above) fastback proposals were seriously considered for production.

cided not to spend any more. A front-drive Thunderbird would be considered again, but not for more than two decades. . .

Unlike McNamara, Iacocca understood the image value of low-volume cars with high-performance and high-style. He supported the Thunderbird Sports Roadster, a sort of low-investment, two-seater revival. How do you make a four-seater into a two-seater without spending much money? By bolting a fiberglass tonneau cover over the back seat! The 25-pound cover, with its aerodynamic headrest fairings, at least provided some concealed luggage space, which the convertible sorely lacked. A set of genuine Kelsey-Hayes wire wheels (optional on other 'Birds) complemented the neoclassic image, but the model proved unpopular; only 1,427 were sold in '62.

The performance-oriented testers at *Car Life* were not as impressed with the Thunderbird as their colleagues at *Motor Trend* had been the year before. ''As automobiles go,'' *Car Life* wrote in July 1962, ''the current Thunderbird is adequate in most respects but not very outstanding.'' They found a 0 to 60 mph time of 12.4 seconds ''disappointing'' and moaned that the T-Bird's springs and shocks were still far too soft to support its sporting image. (As the editors noted, Chrysler endowed its contemporary 300-H with front springs 24 percent stiffer than the Thunderbird's; the hot Chrysler's rear springs were 33 percent stiffer.) Brake fade was still a problem. But *Car Life* did allow that their Sports Roadster's heavy unit body made it ''undoubtedly the stiffest convertible we have ever tested.'' And they had no difficulty divining the Thunderbird's true mission: ''On the highway it's quiet and smooth, in front of your house it will turn your neighbors green with envy.

However, even the generally laudatory *Motor Trend* was starting to lose patience with the 'Bird's ''less than average performance and [handling] like a land-locked whale.'' They allowed, however, that high-speed float was much reduced from '61 and added, ''The ride is also one of the quietest we've experienced in any car.''

To improve the T-Bird's performance, Iacocca had backed the triple-carb, high-compression (10.5:1 vs. 9.6:1) ''M-series'' engine for '62, producing 340 bhp at 5000 rpm. Torque was not increased significantly (430 vs. 427 lb-ft) but the torque peak climbed up the scale from 2800 to 3200 rpm. The country-clubbers yawned, and only a few hundred were built. A new vinyl-top option with fake landau irons proved far more popular. Iacocca's enthusiasm for performance cars was clearly not shared by the average 'Bird buyer, and the market was driving Ford's ''personal car'' slowly but inexorably down Luxury Lane. The triple-carb option vanished in '63.

That year, the T-Bird was treated to another new grille and to a somewhat dubious crease pressed into its front fenders and doors. The Sports Roadster limped on, in spite of minuscule sales. The big news, instead, was the Limited Edition Landau—the ''Princess Grace'' Thunderbird in the vernacular—introduced to the press in Monaco by movie actress Grace Kelly, the reigning Princess. The ''Princess Grace,'' of which 2,000 were built, featured a white-and-rose trim scheme with fake rosewood interior highlights.

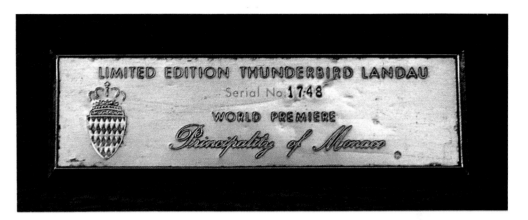

This is Number 1 of a limited international edition
(Number 2 to 2,000 could be yours. See your Ford Dealer)

Thunderbird
LIMITED EDITION LANDAU
Première à Principauté de Monaco. Janvier 1963

Factory-installed dashboard plaque (above) identifies Don Taylor's 1963 Thunderbird Limited Edition Landau as no. 1748 of the 2000 that were built. These ''Princess Grace'' Thunderbirds featured white leather upholstery, rosewood applique (instead of bright metal) on the dash and console, and white paint with a rose vinyl top.

31

1964 Thunderbird Convertible, owned by Robert Gehrke. "Coved" rear seat (right) was created by interior stylist Art Querfeld.

In the marketplace, the Thunderbird had a real rival by 1963; Buick sold 40,000 Rivieras that year, a strong start against the Thunderbird's sales volume of 63,313 units.

The Thunderbird was completely reskinned for 1964, although its floor pan, running gear, and driveline continued unchanged. Boyer described the '64 as a marriage of the '58-'60 and '61-'63 themes, noting especially the tail end, where the '58-'60 dual-pod look was updated, cleaned up, and squared-off for mid-Sixties tastes. Oros disagrees with this interpretation. "We absolutely did not go back to the '58," he stated. "We developed horizontal pods but not intentionally

to pick up from the '58." Oros prefers to think of the '64 purely as an extrapolation of the '61-'63 theme, retaining a similar front end and "aerodynamic" shape.

Halderman reported that a fastback version was seriously considered, even approved at one time, although it was canned before it reached production. A restyled Sports Roadster that did reach the showrooms was now listed simply as an option for convertibles, not as a separate model. Fewer than 50 were sold. (Despite this less-than-glorious success, aftermarket suppliers have since concocted similar tonneau kits for 1958-60 as well as '61-'63 and '64-'66 Thunderbirds.)

Fiberglass model (top) and sketches (above), all from 1961-62, illustrate how the 1964 Thunderbird evolved from the '61-63 theme.

The body engineers expanded the trunk of the '64 'Bird to 11.5 cubic feet—and the convertible top still took up all of it. For added convenience, though, the doors now opened *past* the front edge of the rear seat. Up front, a dramatically monstrous visor shielded the sort of gee-whiz instrument panel that could still arouse jealousy in Tokyo today. (Carped *Car and Driver* in August: ''. . . here in four-wheeled form is the embodiment of the strange desire to fabricate an immensely complicated device that in essence does nothing in any practical sense.'' But, then, the *C/D* editors suggested in the same report that the Thunderbird's novel door-ajar warning light and vanguard power door locks were silly gimmicks, too.) The car's one true engineering advance was flow-through ventilation—another Mercedes-Benz first that made its domestic debut in the Thunderbird. Ford sold 82,865 '64 T-Birds, the best showing since 1960.

The Thunderbird changed little for 1965. Gene Bordinat, formerly the head of Lincoln-Mercury studio, had replaced Walker as Design VP in 1962. Bordinat's first concern was the all-new '65 full-size line, then the most thoroughly re-engineered Ford cars since 1949. Recalled Halderman:

I got transferred out of Advanced Design, and moved to the Ford studio, and started working on this all-new Ford with Joe Oros. He was there morning, noon, and night with me. So we had to do a two-door, a four-door, a wagon. And right in the middle of all that—God, we were up to here!—along came an assignment to do a Thunderbird *and* to do a Mustang. . .We did all that at the same time, all of it together.

Ultimately, the designers were able to do little more for the '65 'Bird than reshuffle the chrome and add a neat set of sequential turn signals at the rear. The latter had been planned for '64, but Ford needed the extra year to work out some reliability bugs—and to lobby some recalcitrant state governments that hadn't greeted the idea with the expected enthusiasm.

The engineers, however, finally cured the T-Bird's brake-fade problem with front disc brakes—the same year that Chevrolet first supplied a disc brake option for the vaunted Corvette. *Motor Trend* didn't get around to testing a disc-brake 'Bird until March 1966, but the intrepid editors were happy with the change. ''A serious shortcoming of previous models,'' they noted, ''has been remedied by the optional front disc brakes. These add new dimensions to T-Bird driving, and greatly lessen the probability of this 4,700 pound pleasure dome interfering with someone else's forward motion.'' Unfortunately, the disc brakes left no room for the lovely Kelsey-Hayes wire wheels, so they had to be dropped from the option list.

The '64 Mustang had at last broken down Ford's edict against painted metal beneath the front bumper. Iacocca and Bordinat both supported more adventurous styling and, as Boyer noted, ''safety advocates'' were already screaming for a uniform bumper height. Purely as a stylist, Boyer welcomed the opportunity to lighten up the T-Bird's

front end for '66 with what he called a "blade-type bumper bar." Halderman wasn't as happy about it: "When we had to put that bumper on it, we cried. . . We thought it destroyed the whole fluid form of the car." Dave Ash worked out the final design, which really proved quite handsome even if it did depart from T-Bird tradition.

No one could argue, however, with the '66 T-Bird's performance. The standard 390-cid V-8 was now rated 315 bhp, despite a slight reduction in compression ratio, from 10.8 to 10.5:1. The option sheet listed a 428-cid monster-motor developing 345 bhp at 4600 rpm.

The bigger engine, of course, was just the harbinger of the bigger 'Bird to come. The chain of events that led to it was indeed ironic: The two-seat Thunderbird had been inspired by General Motors' Corvette; but the four-seater had proven to be a completely new type of product, for which GM had no response until the Buick Riviera of 1963. By 1966, however, the Riviera was already wearing the fruits of its first redesign, the Oldsmobile Toronado had appeared, and the front-drive Cadillac Eldorado was looming on the horizon. None of these bulkier pretenders would ever outsell the Thunderbird in any given year, yet their very existence seemed to pressure Ford into building its 'Birds ever bigger through the next 10 years.

Today, even Ford insiders admit that 1966 marked the end of the Thunderbird's youth and the onset of its uncertain middle age.

1966 Thunderbird Convertible, owned by John E. Taylor. Slimmer front bumper and ultra-clean lines distinguish the last of the "compact" four-seaters.

TWO DOORS OR FOUR

1967-88

THE T-BIRD'S NEXT EVOLUTION," wrote Boyer, "was not as apparent as the 1958-1961 theme combination had been."

At least eight distinct styling themes were proposed for the '67 Thunderbird, all of which progressed at least as far as full-size clay. Not one of them possessed the interest, character or focus of *any* Thunderbird that had gone before. By the mid-Sixties, the 'Bird had clearly lost its way. The design finally chosen for 1967 was, not surprisingly, a compromise. Dave Ash created its giant-jet-scoop front end, perhaps borrowing the theme from the wild, two-wheel Ford Gyron show car concocted by Ford's professional visionary, Alex Tremulis. The rest of the '67 'Bird can be credited to Boyer, who wrote that he and his crew were trying to achieve "very smooth sheet metal workouts typified by the roof quarter areas flowing unbroken into the rear quarters and deck lids." None of which was apparent once the roof was covered with the requisite slab of vinyl.

A handsome fiberglass model from June 1965 showed this theme but with a more radical taper to the front and rear ends and a racy, falling roofline. Somehow, the car had bulked up more on the way to production than a weight lifter on the way to the Olympics.

Worse still, it had lost its ability to generate controversy.

Iacocca wanted to offer the Thunderbird as a four-door. The idea was not new; Ford has photos of a full-size, four-door clay model based on recognizable 1958 T-Bird styling themes. Its numerical code

"Bunkie [Knudsen] thought the 'Bird had kind of lost track of where it was going. . . . I don't doubt that he would have liked the 'Bird eventually to have been a much more compact, better, functional car. . . ."

—Paul Preuss, Manager Ford Product and Technology Public Affairs

indicates that it was sculpted in September 1955 (perhaps at McNamara's behest?). It has a tight, close-coupled greenhouse, with a short rear door quite like that of the '67 production model. Almost 10 years later, Lincoln-Mercury stylists experimented with renderings of a formal, four-door Cougar. It is difficult to know whether this inspired the Thunderbird's designers or vice versa. Boyer writes only that his crew developed a full-size rendering of a four-door Thunderbird that charmed both Iacocca and Bordinat instantly.

Halderman recalled a consensus to the effect that the Thunderbird had to grow bigger to keep potential buyers satisfied. That's not surprising, given the sheer mass of the T-Bird's newfound competitors. The Riviera and Toronado both rode on 119-inch wheelbases, and the Eldorado on 120. Stretching the Thunderbird to 115 inches (117 for the four-door) must have seemed conservative by comparison.

At the same time, the Ford engineers abandoned unitized construction and, for the first time since 1957, returned to a separate frame for the Thunderbird. Langworth attributed this step to cost-cutting, but the fact that all 14 rubber body mounts were located either in front of or behind the passenger compartment suggests that isolation from road noise might also have had something to do with the decision.

The single-lower-arm suspension remained up front but with the coil spring relocated to the lower arm, of course. The T-Bird's live rear axle was now located by two trailing links, with a single anti-torque link to the right of the differential and a Panhard rod behind it—standard practice on full-size Fords since 1965. In fact, most of the T-Bird's running gear, and even the front- and rear-end sections

Preceding page: 1967 Thunderbird Two-Door Landau, owned by Alice Grace Kalash. This page: Among the many styling proposals for the '67 'Bird was this full-size rendering of a pillarless four-door (above), dated May 1964. It appears to have been based on a two-door clay (top) from March of that year.

of its frame, were shared with Ford's full-size sedans.

The 315-bhp 390-cid engine remained standard in the engine bay, with the 345-bhp 428 as an option. However, by revising the automatic shift pattern to P-R-N-2-D-1, with a lockout for N and 1, the driveline engineers made manual override exceptionally fast and easy.

Incredibly, all of this apparent compromise resulted in a better automobile, one that was, according to *Car Life* (February 1967), "slicker, quieter, smoother and more comfortable than its predecessors." By November 1966, *Car and Driver* had already pitted the new four-door Thunderbird against its most expensive rival, the Cadillac Eldorado. At 12 seconds flat, the 'Bird lost the 0 to 60-mph race by 0.3-second, only to even it out in the quarter mile at 17.8 seconds to the Eldo's 17.9. Then the Thunderbird positively clobbered the Caddy in *C/D*'s brake test, stopping from 80 mph in 330 feet against the Eldorado's 386. Not bad, for two-thirds the price.

In the ensuing two years, little changed in the Thunderbird department. At the beginning of the 1968 model year, Ford's heavier-duty 360-bhp, 429-cid V-8 replaced the 428 as the optional engine, becoming standard by December. In 1969, two-door models were given a lower, stiffer suspension that improved handling. *Car Life* noted in February that the Thunderbird was not as stable as the contemporary

Riviera, though it beat the Buick in adhesion. In the market, Thunderbird sales dropped from 77,956 in 1967 to 49,272 in 1969, while the Grand Prix, Riviera and Toronado made significant gains.

Changes were on the way.

Along with a new Thunderbird, Ford had acquired a new president in 1967: Semon E. "Bunkie" Knudsen, fresh from GM, where he had revitalized both Chevrolet and Pontiac. Paul M. Preuss, currently manager of Product and Technology Public Affairs, learned quickly that Bunkie had a different style than his peers:

I remember the Daytona 500 right after he joined the company. I was so used to somewhat reserved executives in those days. When Lee Roy Yarborough came from behind on the last lap, Bunkie was jumping up and down and pounding on the table and hollering. And I said, "What a difference!"

Knudsen loved cars—big cars, powerful cars, cars with dramatic good looks. He had little patience for Ford's various styling proscriptions, nor the conservative practicality they represented. For example, to simplify manufacturing, Ford engineers had forbidden any stationary sheetmetal between the engine hood and the grille. Some GM models, on the other hand, used "hatch hoods" behind a "grille opening panel" (g.o.p.), which could be easily replaced each year for a new front-end appearance. Bunkie consistently went to bat for Styling, to get what the engineers insisted wasn't possible. "In fact," recalled Halderman, "when we told him that [an engineer said] that something wasn't feasible, he'd say, 'You have the guy here next week and let me talk to him.' And that's about all it took. Usually, the engineer never showed up."

To Knudsen, however, the big-but-sporty Thunderbird was something of an enigma. As Preuss remembered:

I think Bunkie thought the 'Bird had kind of lost track of where it was going. That's when he tried to get more distinctive styling into it . . . I don't doubt that he would have liked the Bird eventually to have been a much more compact, better, functional car . . . It was almost aimed at Cadillac, and I think Bunkie would have aimed it right on the Pontiac [Grand Prix].

Halderman added:

He questioned the Thunderbird a lot . . . Why we have it in the company? Where does it fit? Who do we sell it to? . . . I think he was trying to sort out in his mind where it really fit in. When he left the company, I don't think he had that solved yet.

However, as Preuss recalled, "I don't think Bunkie was above having our cars look more like GM cars." And an integral part of Dr. Bunkie's prescription for more dramatic styling was a sort of prominent, pointed prow that Ford insiders still call a "Bunkie Beak."

Urged on by Knudsen, Ford stylists explored several themes for a Torino-based T-Bird for 1970—all sporting proud "Bunkie Beaks," of course. The high hip line on the definitive car seems to have been inherited from these studies. Halderman thinks that Bunkie may have arrived too late in the program to have effected a platform change, but he isn't sure. For whatever reason, the '70 Thunderbird debuted with a suitably dramatic new skin, but little mechanical change. Most significantly, the engineers had lowered the suspension again (by a visible 1.4 inches) and re-tuned it for radial tires.

Pitted against the Riviera and Toronado in a December 1970 *Motor Trend* comparison test, the essentially unchanged '71 Thunderbird paradoxically rode harder but rolled more in turns than its GM rivals, while once again proving the merit of its vastly superior brakes.

Bunkie's sojourn at Ford was brief; Henry II fired him on September 11, 1969. Personality conflicts with Iacocca are generally acknowledged as the cause. Langworth credits the next generation of Thunderbird—the biggest 'Bird of them all—to Iacocca's marketing savvy. But Halderman claimed that it, too, was part of Bunkie's legacy, "even though he left before [it] hit the road." Knudsen had already approved not only the 1972 styling theme but also the 1973 face-lift that would carry the T-Bird through 1976.

The '72 Thunderbird shared its chassis and, indeed, most of its body as well with the Continental Mark IV, riding on a whopping wheelbase of 120.4 inches (a full foot-and-a-half longer than the first T-bird's 102 inches)! The new chassis gave the 'Bird another new rear suspension system, still with trailing links below the live axle but now with two semi-trailing anti-torque links above. The latter were splayed 90 degrees apart to control sway, GM-style.

While the T-Bird had never been completely unique, it had never shared quite so much with another Ford product. Once again, however, Halderman recalled that the course was clear at the time:

> Every time . . . we made it bigger, it seemed it sold a little better and broadened its appeal a little more . . . And it couldn't go smaller. It had to demand the price that we were getting for these cars and had to be about that size. Basically, it was sistered with the Mark because it was the best package. It seemed to be the right seating arrangement. And it picked up a lot of common features with the Mark.

And even if the concept was Bunkie's, salesman Iacocca endorsed it wholeheartedly. Halderman continued:

> Iacocca felt very strongly about that car, the prestige Ford Division car. In size, the bigger it got, the better he liked it. He had no gumption about trying to keep it smaller. It seems that every pound was better.

As usual, Iacocca's guess had been right. In 1973, Thunderbird sales rode an industry-wide crest to peak again at 87,269. And though

Gale Halderman, now director of Large and Luxury Exteriors, has contributed to every Thunderbird from 1958 to the present.

More 1964 proposals for the '67 Thunderbird, ranging from reconstructed rocket ship to arrogant pseudo-Lincoln

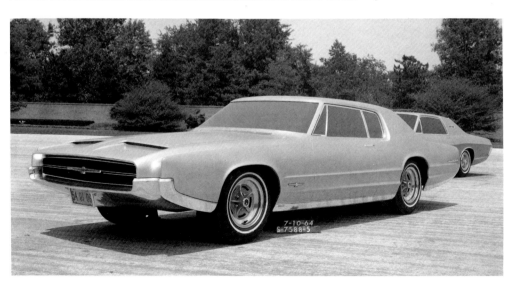

Ford President Semon E. "Bunkie" Knudsen inspired the extroverted look of the '70-76 Thunderbirds.

Thunder for sale: 2 doors or 4.

Fly any way you like with the Bird. 2 doors or 4. Buckets or full-width front seats. Room for 4, 5, or 6. With beautiful standards only the Bird offers as standard. All this, and a hot new Thunder Jet 429 cu. in. V-8 to flash you from where you are to where you're going. What are you waiting for? Get your kind of thunder at your Ford Dealer's now!

'68 Thunderbird
unique in all the world

1968 Thunderbird Four-Door Landau, owned by Ford Motor Company

the rising price of gasoline—as well as that of the cars themselves—had eroded this figure to 36,578 by 1976, the T-Bird continued to out-sell the Toronado and Riviera, year after year.

Even so, the Thunderbird still finished consistently behind GM's smaller, mid-size specialty cars, the Pontiac Grand Prix and Chevrolet Monte Carlo. Ford's tepid response, the Gran Torino Elite, had failed to establish an image. (Halderman called it "a Monte Carlo-fighter [done] with mirrors.") Ford's mid-size lineup was due for a major revision in 1977, just as the Federal government was tightening its Corporate Average Fuel Economy (CAFE) requirements. Ford management realized that it could kill at least two large stones with one medium-size 'Bird.

Boyer had departed for Ford Australia in the summer of '73, leaving Halderman in charge of the Luxury and Intermediate Studio. By this time, the Thunderbird had, for all practical purposes, ceased to exist as a separate program or department. Halderman worked on an entire line of mid-size coupes, sedans and wagons to be sold with minor trim, taillight and g.o.p. variations as the Ford LTD II and Mercury Cougar. One of the coupes had to be a Thunderbird. Another had to be a Cougar XR-7, a Thunderbird equivalent for Lincoln-Mercury.

To enhance the Thunderbird's tenuous identity, Halderman's crew chose a truly outrageous combination of roof-pillar and window shapes, giving the impression of a bold, sheet metal "basket handle" sweep-ing up and over a thin-section, usually vinyl-covered roof. The lower body was crisp and lean, at least compared with that of its immediate ancestors, and the tail end echoed the old Thunderbird "dual pod" theme. The result was, at least, distinctive.

"We were trying to offer two cars basically the same size and appealing to almost the same customer," Halderman said, "so we wanted to make the cars [Thunderbird and XR-7] totally different in terms of . . . the basket handle versus a conventional C-pillar."

Like it or not, you had to admit that the new 'Bird looked different. "It has a taut, linear shape," wrote *Car and Driver* in December '76, "with the sort of bold styling gestures usually seen only on show cars." For the first time in a decade, drama and controversy had returned to Thunderbird styling.

Performance returned as well. The chassis configuration was un-changed, although all the components were new and lighter, and the body was again unitized. The standard engine was a mild-mannered, yet thoroughly adequate, 302-cubic-inch V-8 producing 130 bhp (Ford had switched from gross to net horsepower ratings in 1972), but *Car and Driver*'s test 'Bird packed the optional 173-bhp, 400-cubic-incher. Weighing 630 pounds less than its ponderous predecessor, the new 'Bird flew from 0 to 60 mph in 11.5 seconds and soared through the quarter mile in 17.9—a close match for any T-Bird of the glorious Sixties, save perhaps the triple-carb '62.

With its wheelbase reduced to 114 inches and a performance sus-pension on its option list, the '77 handled better than any 'Bird before it, as well. ". . . body roll angle is tightly controlled," reported *C/D*. "You can nip through the suburban switchbacks with aplomb in this

At Knudsen's urging, Ford stylists explored some radical themes for a smaller Thunderbird. These studies (top left and above left), from 1968-69, clearly influenced the 1970 production model (above). Ultimately, however, the '72 'Bird grew *bigger*, perched atop a Continental Mark IV chassis. This 1972 Thunderbird (left), owned by George Watts, is the one-millionth automobile to bear the famous name.

machine. And even more important, the suspension has a feeling of discipline you don't find in every Detroit car.'' Best of all, by building the 'Bird on a mass-market chassis, Ford was able to reduce the base price by an incredible 35 percent, to just $5,063. Dearborn's dealers moved 318,140 Thunderbirds out the doors in 1977, which was a record by far. Then, just to prove it was no fluke, they topped that number in 1978, with 352,751 sales, still an all-time high. And they nearly did it one more time in '79.

By then, however, the 400-cid engine option was gone, and even the downsized Thunderbird appeared to be carrying a little too much Thunderbulk. For 1980, in the name of fuel efficiency, Ford abandoned the most popular Thunderbird of all time.

Its replacement was based on Ford's ubiquitous Fox chassis, a mid-size, unit-body platform that had debuted in 1978 under the unassuming Ford Fairmont and Mercury Zephyr sedans. Mechanically conservative, its live rear axle was located by two trailing and two semi-trailing links; its front end rode on a hybrid strut suspension with coil springs mounted on broad-based lower wishbones. Its steering gear was rack-and-pinion, promising some handling potential. For Thunderbird duty, Ford stuffed its engine bay with a new 255-cid V-8, although the 302 was still available. A 200-cid six (the first six ever in a Thunderbird) joined the option list in the spring.

The result wasn't all bad. Somehow, the engineers found three more inches of rear-seat knee room in the significantly smaller package. The trimmer size improved handling, while acceleration with the 302 just about matched that of the previous 'Bird with the 400. Still, *Car and Driver* gave the new Thunderbird only a lukewarm welcome in July 1980:

. . . it's the closest the T-Bird has ever come to being a driver's car. By all accounts, it's easily the best T-Bird of the last 25 years. But . . . for all its improvements it's only drawn even with the competition . . .

1976 Thunderbird (top), and 1977 Thunderbird Hardtop (above), both owned by Kennedy-Haldeman Ford. Without its basket-handle roof, the '77 'Bird would have closely resembled the two-door LTD II—as can be seen in this fiberglass proposal from 1974 (right). Fairmont-based T-Bird study from 1976 (far right) reached production as the '78 Fairmont Futura.

Ford designers envisioned a radical wedge theme for the 1980 Thunderbird (above), but Iacocca wanted a more conservative look. Four-door revival (far left, with designer Kyu Kim) made it as far as fiberglass—but all of the '80-'82 'Birds that actually rolled off the lines in Chicago (bottom left) and Lorain, Ohio were two-door sedans. New 108.4-inch wheelbase didn't quite reflect the 102-inch original (left).

1983 Thunderbird Turbo Coupe (above and opposite), owned by Ford Motor Company

Allen Ornes (below), along with John Aiken, led the design team that transformed the Thunderbird from a glittering box to a dazzling bullet.

Without doubt, the most disappointing aspect of the '80 'Bird was its boxy, bulky styling; somehow, its body always looked too big for its 108.4-inch wheelbase.

According to Allen Ornes, currently a Ford design executive in the Large and Luxury Interiors Studio, the '80 'Bird was designed to please Iacocca's taste more than anything else. "In the studios," he said, "we designers just felt it was all wrong." During 1976-77, Fritz Mayhew and Allen Ornes were the managers assigned to develop advanced proposals that would become the themes for the 1980 Thunderbird and Cougar. The sharp, crisp, folded-paper school of design, supported by aerodynamic testing, was reaching its zenith and, having just worked on the 1979 Mustang and Capri, the designers were ready to apply a similarly dynamic and wedgy look to the Thunderbird. The front end was to be no higher than it had to be to accommodate the rectangular sealed-beam headlights of the day and would feature a low, flush grille.

"But that," said Halderman, "was totally in reverse of what Iacocca wanted in this car:

I wish you could have seen the original '80 car. It was much smaller, sleeker, lower, and just didn't pass Iacocca's test of size, luggage volume, prestige. He didn't want it to be sleek, he wanted it to be an elegant-looking, an expensive-looking *box* . . . He wasn't anti-aero, except he said, "I will buy any aero improvements you want to make in a car, but don't ever let me see it."

Halderman said they had "a lot of reviews" on the design. He related one instance when the designers had found they could achieve a significant improvement in coefficient of drag by lowering the front edge of the hood by one inch. But Iacocca wouldn't hear of it.

One memorable 1980 advertisement showed the latest T-Bird parked on the edge of a lake; reflected in the still water was a 1956 two-seater. "The Thunder's Still There," exhorted the headline. But, like the car itself, the advertisement all too clearly reflected only the desperation of the times. Sales plummeted, while layoffs decimated the entire industry. The Thunderbird—and the Ford Motor Company—needed a new flight plan, and fast.

In 1961, the Continental had been saved from oblivion when it adopted a Thunderbird styling theme; now the time had come for Lincoln to return the favor. Before that could happen, however, some new personalities had to climb the corporate totem pole.

Henry Ford II shocked the industry by dismissing Iacocca in October 1978, then retired one year later on October 1, 1979. Philip Caldwell, previously the head of Ford's overseas operations, succeeded Henry II as chairman. For the first time, the Ford Motor Company was led by someone outside of the Ford family. In March 1980, Caldwell appointed ace product planner Don Petersen president and chief operating officer. Jack J. Telnack was then executive director of the North American Mid-Size Exterior and Interior studios.

According to Ornes, the 1983 Thunderbird was originally expected to be "just a slightly softened evolution" of the crisp and boxy '80-'82 car. Meanwhile, the newly downsized Lincoln Town Car and Continental Mark VI were off to a slow start in the sales wars. With the Federal government threatening ever-stricter CAFE regulations, Ford's product planners realized that the *next* Town Car and Mark might have to be built on the even smaller Fox platform—further reducing their sales appeal along with their size.

The designers feared that the Mark, especially, would lose what little remained of its character and personality in another round of downsizing. So Telnack's studio (led by Ornes and John Aiken) conceived a styling theme that would still look elegant and expensive on an extended Fox platform. Abandoning the slab-sided, straight-edged forms that Ford had favored for years, they first created a clay model and then a fiberglass model using very rounded, flowing forms, with flush glass and the strong, functional character of a European touring coupe. Seeing it more as a "driver's car," than the traditional Mark, they called it, informally, the "Aero Luxury Car."

Petersen, looking for new design directions, enthusiastically backed the Aero Luxury Car for development and supported it for production. Ultimately, it reached the public in late 1983 as the 1984 Lincoln Mark VII. First, however, Telnack's team derived a new Thunderbird from the Aero Luxury Car, as well. As Halderman remembered:

We wanted to give the Thunderbird a bold image and a new look, a fresh start. And that didn't come easy. If I recall, we did several proposals and at the eleventh hour we pulled in a fiberglass car that was around. This was the Aero Luxury Car, quickly modified into a Thunderbird for a weekend customer clinic. When it was uncovered, the people applauded and we had a 1983 Thunderbird, in June of 1980.

This softer, more aerodynamic form undoubtedly shocked the corporate conservatives, but it continued to fare well in styling clinics, generating strong, emotional responses. The aerodynamic Thunderbird actually reached the market more than six months ahead of the historic Lincoln that had inspired it.

"It was the time for the whole company to regenerate itself," said Ornes, "and that vehicle, the aero Thunderbird, was the one that took the lead and became the symbol of our new identity." The same styling theme inspired the Mercury Cougar and Topaz and the compact Ford Tempo, which were designed at the same time as the Thunderbird and released the following year. Ford had committed itself, irreversibly, to a new styling direction and a new corporate culture.

Under the '83 T-Bird's sleek new skin was the same Fox chassis—not necessarily a bad thing—but shortened to 104 inches in wheelbase for sportier proportions. The only engine offered initially was a 3.8-liter (232-cid) V-6 developing an uninspiring 118 bhp. By the spring of 1983, however, the 302 V-8 had returned, along with the exciting new "Turbo Coupe," motivated by a turbocharged and fuel-injected

1988 Thunderbird Turbo Coupe, owned by Rhett Ricart. Air-to-air intercooler, among other changes, boosted power output from 145 to 190 bhp. Note Programmed Ride Control actuators on top of the shock towers.

four. This sohc unit displaced 2.3 liters (140 cid) and boasted 145 bhp at 4600 rpm, which is expected now but was impressive then. The Turbo Coupe package included stiffer springs and gas-filled shocks for handling, four of the latter at the rear, to compensate for the less-than-perfect location of the Fox's live axle.

Road & Track rediscovered the Thunderbird in January 1983, clocking a Turbo Coupe from 0 to 60 mph in 9.7 seconds and through the quarter mile in 17.1. "To say this car is the best Thunderbird in years is a dramatic understatement," the testers concluded, adding, "The Turbo Coupe's handling and responsiveness are right up there with the best of its class." In July, *Car and Driver* dropped all pretense of restraint while describing the Turbo Coupe experience as "a glorious, ecstatic, hot-diggity, oh boy! flush of wonderfulism that hasn't come shooting out of a Thunderbird's innards since the mid-1950s." Abetted, no doubt, by the new 'Bird's aero shape, the *C/D* testers clocked a true top speed of 123 mph, probably faster than a showroom-stock 'Bird had ever flown before.

The Thunderbird continued essentially unchanged through 1984. For 1985, the designers fashioned a handsome new instrument panel to replace the bluff, square-shouldered dash that the '83-'84 'Bird had inherited from its '80-'82 ancestor. Now the gentle, flowing shapes of the Thunderbird's exterior were continued on the inside as well.

I still remember flogging an (unchanged) '86 Turbo Coupe through the countryside west of Princeton, New Jersey; the big four growled like a rock-polishing machine, but no combination of exuberant cor-

nering and torturous pavement seemed able to upset the 'Bird's tight grip on the road, nor could it elicit the slightest flex or complaint from its rock-solid unit body. The contemporary Chevrolet Monte Carlo SS, Oldsmobile Cutlass 4-4-2 and Buick Regal Grand National all offered smoother engines, but their whippy chassis and brutish suspensions felt positively antediluvian in comparison.

A new grille and taillights were all that was originally scheduled for the '87 Thunderbird, but by the time the designers were finished, every panel save the engine hood and front fenders had been changed. Combined with engineering revisions, the 'Bird's new look cost Ford $250 million. This was a hefty investment in a car that would be produced for only two more years.

At first glance, the 1987 Thunderbird appeared to be a huge step in the wrong direction, with its exaggerated front overhang and its abundance of fussy detail. Dave Turner, who was a studio manager in 1983-84, admitted that, after the terrific '83-'86 design, the '87-'88 cars were something of a compromise, an attempt to take the aero look another half-step ahead without changing the platform. "You couldn't look at architecture on the '87," he said. "All you could do was add a new facia." Still, Turner, who is now director of Advanced Concepts and Industrial Design, believes that the '87 'Bird represented a necessary transition between the '83-'86 cars and the all-new '89:

> The goals of the '87 car were to modernize it with flush glass . . . to start picking up on a little bit of this feeling that the Taurus and Sable have . . . You see, the Taurus and Sable have kind of a flushness about them. It was also intended to look unique a little bit so that people realized there was a change.

Turner defended the '87 T-Bird's fussy taillights (though not enthusiastically) as a sort of designer's rebellion against the trend toward pure simplicity and function in this area, an attempt to return to the days when taillights were distinctive, without returning to the heavy-handed sculpture and chrome that had made them so.

The addition of an intercooler, along with major refinements to the intake and exhaust system, boosted peak power to 190 bhp and peak torque to 240 lb-ft. Changes to the chassis were less obvious but just as important. The engineers added disc brakes at the rear wheels, along with an anti-lock system. New lower control arms altered the front suspension geometry, while electronically controlled shock absorbers allowed the chassis crew to substitute softer springs. Thus revised, the '87 Thunderbird garnered *Motor Trend*'s Car of the Year Award. In October 1986, *Car and Driver* recorded an improved top speed of 137 mph but expressed reservations about the T-Bird's adjustable suspension and rough-running engine. I echoed the same sentiments in *Road & Track* in August '87.

As Turner pointed out, however, the '87-'88 T-Birds were necessary transitions. An all-new Thunderbird, the most daring, controversial and exciting Thunderbird yet, was already complete and awaiting its debut before a single '87 left the showroom floor.

THE NEW GENERATION

1989-

DAVE TURNER was a studio manager in the middle of 1983, when planning began for project MN12: a platform for the 1989 Thunderbird. Even as the avant-garde Aero-Bird of 1983-88 was inserting a tentative toe into an initially indifferent marketplace, Ford was already designing its more radical replacement.

Like the Taurus and Sable before it, the latest Thunderbird constitutes an historic gamble, a radical departure from the conventional wisdom so cherished by Ford's competitors. General Motors spent over $5 billion developing its GM10 chassis, a mild-mannered, versatile, front-wheel-drive platform that will carry the General's mid-size sedans, vans and specialty cars alike into the Nineties. In startling contrast, Ford, already the possessor of the most widely acclaimed mid-size, front-drive platform in U.S. history, chose to create an all-new, *rear*-drive chassis for the Thunderbird, 5½ inches longer in wheelbase and nearly 500 pounds heavier than its GM10 competitors.

As if this deviation weren't sufficiently daring, Ford also offers the high-profile Thunderbird SC, packing a heavy-duty, 3.8-liter V-6 stoked by the first positive-displacement supercharger ever to pump quantities of atmosphere into an American production car, and large quantities they are, too. Combined with sophisticated electronic controls for both steering and suspension, this 210-bhp mega–motor promises effortless triple-digit performance for around $20,000.

Ford management carefully considered building a "Taurus T-Bird"

> **The first thing you do is you get the people-part of the car right. . . . Be responsible about [that], and then let that lead you to the design.**
>
> —Dave Turner, director of Advanced Concepts and Industrial Design, Ford Motor Company

on a shared front-drive platform. After all, the '89 Thunderbird was spawned when the age of big-engine performance still seemed to be forever past and when a front-wheel driveline could easily have handled any plant that might conceivably supply the power. According to Turner, the MN12 "began life as a front-drive car that was brought all the way through Design Staff [which handles advanced concepts and early feasibility studies] and almost to the point of being executed in North American Design, when it was switched around to a rear-drive car." That was still in 1983.

To appreciate the moment of that decision, said Turner, one must understand the difference between "styling" and "design." In automotive parlance, the former is superficial, dealing chiefly with decorating an existing shape; the latter implies the creation of new shapes from the pavement up. "Sculpture, graphics and the details are separable from the proportions and architecture," Turner explained. "The proportions and architecture are *inseparable* from the interior package and . . . the essence of the vehicle." It is along these very lines that the '89 Thunderbird departs significantly from even its recent aerodynamic forbears.

Allen Ornes stressed how the "anatomy" of the MN12 made the designers' jobs easy. Given the perfect proportions of the platform, he said, echoing the sentiments of those who designed the very first Thunderbird, "It's almost impossible to do an ugly car."

Ted Finney agreed. He was a senior designer at the start of the MN12 program and has since been promoted to design manager and then design executive. Working under Halderman, and ultimately un-

der Fritz Mayhew (chief design executive of North American Design), Finney was involved with the earliest concept sketches, and at the beginning of the program, it was his responsibility not only to have the various proposals shown to management but also to supervise the construction of fiberglass models and, later still, full-metal prototypes.

The strength of the MN12, according to Finney, is its distinctiveness, as well as the total integration of its design:

> Before you even get close to the cars, they make a statement. The cars look sleeker [than the GM10 cars]. They look more distinctive. They look terrific moving through traffic. You can lose a GM10 car: "What was that? I don't know." You're not going to lose one of the MN12s. . . . [They've] got tremendous presence. The sheetmetal looks good with the glass, which looks good with the tires, which look good with everything.

Finney said that, in the planning stages, the designers expressed their desire for a "fast windshield, low cowl, longer wheelbase, shorter overhangs" and a lower hoodline than would be possible with all the car's innards stuffed between the front wheels. He wasn't sure whether the MN12 design would have been as successful had it been based on a front-drive platform, but he believed that the 1989 Thunderbird looked the way it did (and the GM10 cars looked the way *they* did) more because of the respective designers' mind-set than the configuration of the chassis:

> If you look at what they did with the sheetmetal and where they decided to go with their overhangs, certainly . . . their feeling for sculpture at the time was different than what our feeling was. We were far more willing to investigate softer shapes and forms; breaking the corners in, for instance, was something we were pioneering at the time, which was something GM simply wasn't doing. They were filling out the cube. They were still making boxes, albeit with some rounder shapes here and there.

In fact, the Thunderbird designers tried out some ideas that were even more aerodynamically radical, with hatchbacks, full rear fender

skirts and "soft wrapped" facias with no apparent bumper shelf. All were rejected in market research. The final design, which was initiated in late 1984, was supported strongly by the response from test groups of potential customers, scoring consistently and significantly better than various alternative proposals. And according to Turner, who is now Ford's director of Advanced Concepts and Industrial Design, "Market research led us to that car, I would say, almost more than we led ourselves to that car."

The only design elements that the new Thunderbird inherited directly from the Taurus/Sable are the standard styling devices Ford employs these days to mask critical body joints: doors that wrap into the roof, for example, and an engine hood that shingles slightly over the top of the headlamps and the front facia (a retreat from Knudsen's troublesome grille-opening-panel front end). And all Ford products now sport a molding where the roof meets the quarter panel, to avoid filling the weld there with lead solder.

More important, however, the Thunderbird inherited from the Taurus/Sable a more functional approach to automobile design. According to Turner:

> In the Taurus and Sable, for the first time, we, as designers, began analyzing what a car really was, what the function of things were. . . . If people don't like dinky knobs on their radio, let's get big knobs on it, and *then* we'll figure out what that does to the design. Let the functions lead you to what the design ought to be.

The MN12 program also perpetuated the team approach to simultaneous engineering of both the product and the manufacturing, servicing and sales processes that Ford pioneered in the Taurus/Sable project. Ironically, it was this very heritage of customer-driven, team-oriented vehicle development that guaranteed that the Thunderbird would share hardly a single nut or bolt of the Taurus' anatomy. The Thunderbird is intended for a different market, and it was engineered accordingly.

Directing the MN12 project for the last two-and-a-half years was Anthony S. Kuchta, program manager for Mid-Size Specialty Programs and a 30-year veteran of Ford Engineering.

Reporting to Kuchta was Bruce M. Kopf, who first became involved with the Thunderbird in 1983 as Ford's advanced vehicle planning manager. One of a very few Ford planners to follow a single project from conception to public introductions, Kopf either chaired or co-chaired the committee that planned the progress of the new T-bird during its five-and-a-half years of development.

The committee itself changed over the years, but it generally consisted of between 35 and 45 product planners, marketing analysts, engineers, designers, cost estimators, manufacturing people, agents and accountants—representing all of the professional fields and viewpoints that must be considered to make an automobile aesthetically, mechanically and commercially successful.

Consumer perceptions were always a paramount concern. "People that buy specialty cars," Kopf emphasized, "care very much about what their image is. *Very* much." The team decided early on that an ultimate-performance version was needed to maintain the T-Bird's youthful and aggressive image: This would be the SC-Thunderbird. And ultimate performance, said Kopf, still demands rear-wheel drive:

It's got better weight distribution, which means it will brake better. . . . There'll be less demand on the front brakes than in a front-drive car. So right there, it's got better braking, all things [being] equal. It's got better acceleration on dry pavement because of the weight transfer on the rear wheels and off the front wheels. In handling, it puts less load on the front tires. It makes the rear do something. So it's spreading the work to both the front and rear tires.

Of course, it also pays the aforementioned dividends in styling. Kopf admitted to one more reason for the rear-drive choice: Ford knew that General Motors would favor front-drive for its next generation of mid-size specialty cars, the cars that would become the GM10 series. Kuchta's team wanted to do things a little differently from the boys at GM.

The choice of a rear-drive layout led inevitably to independent rear suspension (irs). Said Kopf:

The irs, for instance, was also a strategic decision; it didn't just fall out of the [design] process. . . . Product planning very much drove irs because of the view that if we brought out an all-new car that was rear drive and had a solid axle, in the face of the

Tauruses and the GM10s and you name it, [it would] run the risk [of being] perceived as old technology. . . . So, from a sales position, we felt that if it was going to be rear drive, it had to have irs. That was a given.

The same team approach was applied to choosing a front suspension. In addition to ride and handling, the committee quantified such parameters as weight, hood height, turning circle and the investment required. Not surprisingly, given the twin priorities of dramatic styling and ultimate performance, the team vetoed the inexpensive strut-type suspension that is still favored by most of the industry. Curiously, though, it also eschewed the traditional double-wishbone system and the sophisticated variations on it that have been developed by the Germans and Japanese, favoring instead an old Ford standby: single lower arms with trailing drag struts.

The classic double wishbone was rejected, explained Jim Kennedy, manager of Specialty Car Development, because it efficiently transmits road shocks to the unit body through its multiple mounting points, whereas the drag-strut suspension allows the front wheels to recede and absorb impacts as they encounter sudden elevations in the road. Modern directional-bushing technology has reduced any resulting bump-steer to a minimum. The little bit of bump harshness that the drag strut transmits to the body is fed into the extreme front of the structure, at least 12 inches farther forward of the passengers than would be the case with double wishbones.

In addition, the SC-Thunderbird incorporates a vastly refined version of the previous Turbo Coupe's Programmed Ride Control. Again, a team effort involving Vehicle Development, Chassis Design and the Electronics Division resulted in the adoption of new algorithms that

Dave Turner, director of Advanced Concepts and Industrial Design

Taurus-based, front-drive T-Bird (below left) was considered as late as 1983. Its hatchback body survived into 1984 (below) before it was vetoed by market research.

make it work as well as it does, endowing the 3,700-pound Thunderbird with surprising grace at speed.

The Thunderbird features other, more subtle engineering advances. Luxury-oriented LX models, as well as the SC, are equipped with speed-variable power steering that uses microchip technology to gradually increase steering effort (and, therefore, feedback) as road speed increases, up to a maximum of 80 mph. To provide extra assistance with emergency maneuvers, the computer constantly monitors the angular speed of the steering wheel and returns full servo assistance if the wheel is turned suddenly at high speed. The fuel tank is tucked safely ahead of the rear axle, and to prevent puncture in even the severest crashes, the drive shaft is designed to telescope on impact.

So Kuchta's team had its ultimate-performance chassis. But the ultimate-performance engine to power it still eluded them.

Market research, said Kopf, indicated that "people aren't as satisfied as we thought they should be with the turbo four," particularly in its automatic incarnation. Balance shafts could have cured the big four's violent shakes but not its limited band of usable torque. Then there was the public perception that four cylinders are just not enough for a luxury car, no matter how civilized or pressurized.

Actually, the Eaton Corporation had approached Ford with its positive-displacement blower as early as 1977. Eaton had been involved with industrial supercharging since 1949, but until the first fuel crisis of 1973, forced induction was not regarded as a valid substitute for cubic inches—at least not for the street.

True, centrifugal superchargers had appeared on the '57 "F-Bird" and on a handful of other performance cars in the Fifties and Sixties, but they had failed to capture the attention of the industry as a whole. When automakers finally took another look at force-fed engines in the Eighties, they turned almost invariably to centrifugal blowers driven by exhaust turbines. Turbochargers thrive on high-rpm, wide-open-throttle driving, making them ideal for Grand Prix racing but less than perfect for driving in a variety of road and traffic conditions.

Superchargers do a much better job of delivering torque at low speed, enhancing the off-the-line and around-town liveliness that most consumers interpret as power. At the high end, the supercharger gives up little to the turbocharger. Noise has been the nemesis of the supercharger, relegating it to the speedway and the drag strip.

Eaton's engineers realized that a smoother delivery of the intake charge would reduce not only noise but also heating. The twin, two-lobed rotors of the traditional Roots blower tend to deliver compressed air in violent pulses; adding a third lobe to each rotor decreased the size of the pulses while increasing their frequency. Then Eaton gave each rotor a 60-degree helical twist, so that as one air pulse is completed, the next has already started. (Extremely tight production tolerances are required so that the rotors nestle close enough to each other to work efficiently when cool and yet do not touch as they heat up and expand.) Working in unison, Vehicle Development, Powertrain Development and Eaton tuned the entire inlet system, including tubes, air cleaner, supercharger ports and intercooler to attenuate super-

charger pulses and achieve a pleasing and powerful sound quality for the installation.

The Thunderbird's 1.5-liter supercharger runs at 2.6 times engine speed—very fast, compared to drag-racing setups—and delivers up to 12 psi of boost to the intake manifold. Parasitic power loss can be as much as 60 bhp at 5000 rpm; however, cruising at 55 mph, the supercharger sips only about half a horsepower.

As part of the MN12 durability program, Ford installed the new supercharged driveline in 20 1988 Thunderbird SC cars and distributed them to police departments around the country. Of these, seven went to the Arizona state police, all with light bars mounted at the extreme rear edge of the roof, where they had the least effect on maximum speed. Three others were pressed into duty by Dearborn's own police force. With obvious relish, Kennedy recounted the time that one of the Arizona cars caught a speeding '87 Turbo Coupe after a 140-mph chase. The Turbo-Coupe driver must have been quite surprised when what appeared to be a normally aspirated '88 T-Bird, chrome grille and all, had no difficulty overtaking him!

Interestingly, while the 90-degree V-6 carries a single balance shaft in transverse installations (i.e. in the Taurus, Sable and Continental), the engineers opted against a balance shaft for the Thunderbird. According to Kennedy, the MN12's more conventional, north-south engine orientation provides better opportunities for isolation. Hydraulic engine mounts weigh less and cost less than balance shafts, and as Kopf confessed, "Obviously, if we can save money, we're going to save money." A die-cast aluminum oil pan, rigidly bolted to the transmission bellhousing, helps matters. The results are satisfactory in the normally aspirated versions. In the supercharged cars, however, some gritty harshness still filters through to the driver above 4500 rpm, along with a busy clatter reminiscent of an old solid-lifter V-8. It seems that 315 lb-ft of torque limits isolation opportunities almost as effectively as front-wheel drive.

By keeping the base and supercharged versions of the 3.8-liter V-6 essentially the same, Ford has achieved significant economies of scale, effectively cutting the number of engines that can be installed in the Thunderbird from three to one. The 5-liter V-8 that powered the '87-'88 Thunderbird Sport was axed before the MN12 program began; its tall intake plenum doesn't even fit under the rakish hood of the '89. Nineteen-eighty-three was still mighty close to the spring of 1979 and the second fuel crisis, when Ford's U.S. automotive operations had finished the year in the red by $1 billion (with a *B!*)—while the Japanese reaped the rewards of better EPA numbers. "A lot of people in the industry," recalled Kopf, "thought [it would be] four cylinders forever. Forget the eights for sure, and they were almost ready to write off the sixes."

To be fair, GM isn't offering any V-8-powered personal luxury cars these days either, unless you count the $24,960 Cadillac Coupe de Ville (and even more expensive Eldorado and Allante). On the other hand, Kopf won't deny that Ford (or GM) might at some time in the future stuff an eight into its new-generation specialty cruisers: "I'm

already getting letters. 'How come you don't have an eight? What's the matter with you?' But they can't go across the street and get one from our friends, either. That probably makes it a little easier. . . . But that, I'm sure, won't last forever. They know that, too. We've just got to be fast on our feet, that's all."

The '89 Thunderbird's styling and mechanical layout were firmly established during 1985; by that time, the '83-'86 Thunderbird was conquering its market, providing needed encouragement back in Dearborn. "At that time," Kopf reported, "we concluded that we were on to something good." The Thunderbird and Cougar together had captured 40 percent of the mid-size specialty market. Typically, Ford and Lincoln-Mercury sales combined account for only 20 percent of the industry. The MN12 obtained management's blessing early in 1986. From that point until October 10, 1988, when production began at Ford's Lorain, Ohio, plant, Kuchta's team was occupied with tooling up the production facilities and selecting the final suspension settings. The '89 T-Bird was officially released for sale on what has become Ford's good-luck day: December 26 in 1988.

The most impressive kudo came from *Motor Trend,* which named the Thunderbird SC its "Car of the Year" for 1989. Only two years before, the Turbo Coupe had copped the same honor (the '58 T-bird was also a "Car of the Year"). Of the SC, *MT* called it "one of the most balanced and controllable cars we've ever driven."

Ford personnel are naturally reluctant to reveal future product plans and don't even comment on speculations. However, it requires no gift of premonition to see that the projected Lincoln Mark model of the early Nineties will be derived from the MN12 platform. One might even speculate that it will be powered by Ford's upcoming 4.6-liter V-8; if the MN12 driveline can handle the 315 lb-ft of torque generated by the supercharged V-6, then there isn't an eight made today that'll scare it.

From there, who knows? As Ford develops the Town Car into more of a world-class *(Auto-) bahn*-burner, it could logically adopt at least the Thunderbird's independent rear suspension, if not the entire T-Bird chassis, suitably stretched; ditto the Crown Victoria and Grand Marquis. At the other end of the product spectrum, recall that the Mustang that has been with us since 1979 is based on a shortened version of the same Fox platform that was shared by both the '80-'82 and '83-'88 Thunderbirds. (Imagine a shortened and supercharged MN12 stalking Camaros in the ponycar market!)

In terms of styling, Finney would say only that future 'Birds will build on the inherent strength of the current design:

I don't see us abandoning the real flowing, sporty looks of the car. I think we've got a lot of momentum built up now. At one time, hearkening way back, "Thunderbird" really meant something. . . . We lost that for a while, and now I think the magic is back.

I think it's going to stay.

THE 35TH ANNIVERSARY THUNDERBIRD

1990

JERRY SENIOR, soft-spoken and superbly dressed, doesn't look old enough to have worked for Ford since 1960—even if he did join the company right out of high school, attending Detroit's Society of Arts and Crafts (now the Center for Creative Studies) at night. "And I'll tell you, I just kept my nose to the grindstone until they made me a car stylist. It was the only thing I could think of, it's all I wanted to do."

Later, his sharp eye for colors and fabrics earned him four years designing Ford's corporate offices. More recently, he said, he's been tagged as the unofficial chief of special editions and anniversary editions. When you see Bill Blass or Jacques Cartier hawking Lincolns adorned with their respective signatures, chances are that it was Jerry Senior who assisted them in picking the colors and fabrics. The last anniversary edition Thunderbird, the 25th in 1980 (medium blue with gray moldings), was his creation. He also designed the America's Cup Town Car and the 20th-Anniversary Cougar.

The new Thunderbird is nothing like the original one. It's grown into a much bigger car. You could fit two '55 T-birds in the new one! Still, I think Ford has done a beautiful job, especially on the interior—that's one of the best they've ever done. Overall, the Thunderbird has changed quite a lot in 35 years, but it's nice that it's still around.

—Franklin Hershey

Typically, North American Design had all but finalized the styling of the '89 Thunderbird SC before Senior was assigned to create a special edition for the 1990 model year. A tight schedule precluded any chance to work out the anniversary design with sketches; Senior had to work directly on a full-size, three-dimensional model. Such full-scale models were in short supply, however, and at the time, only 12 hand-built Thunderbird SC's existed, all serving engineering, research and promotional duty. No one would surrender one for experimentation in the color and trim studio. Finally, Senior convinced North American Design to release a fiberglass model. Then he went to work with a team of Ford craftsmen to turn his ideas into paint, tape, and upholstery.

Senior had nothing to do with the '89 Thunderbird's basic shape, nor with the wheels, skirts, air dams, and other embellishments that distinguish the muscular SC. Still, his respect for the car's extraordinary design integrity initially frustrated his efforts. How does one improve on such an *objet d'art?*

This car is relatively stark. The shape, the design is its strength. I had a problem doing an anniversary car because it's [already] such a perfect shape and such a beautiful, well-balanced design. It took me a long time to get started on it. . . . I didn't want to degrade the car in any way. I didn't want to do anything to it, because I liked it that much.

Once black was chosen as the basic color, Senior shunned the obvious red pinstriping in favor of a truly startling color that Ford calls "radiant blue." "The other thing that was important to me," he explained,

was that Ford Division traditionally is blue and the Mercury division is red. So I felt the accent on the car should reflect that tradition. I tried to do that. But you'll notice that this is kind of a "fashion" blue; it's not your run-of-the-mill blue. It's almost purple.

The blue striping harmonizes with the car's blue Ford oval badges, which appeared for the first time on a Thunderbird in 1989.

The side skirts and front and rear air dams are standard Thunderbird SC pieces; Senior gave them a unique look by having them painted "titanium" silver instead of body color. Likewise, the SC's striking cast wheels are painted black for the anniversary edition in a process developed by Reynolds Aluminum in Italy. In fact, the only pieces on the exterior of the car that are actually unique are the winged cloisonne 35th-anniversary badges on the front fenders. To discourage thieves (or would-be future collectors who try to convert standard SCs into 35th Anniversary Edition cars), the badges are designed to disintegrate if removed.

Inside, Senior specified a black environment, including seats with leather bolsters and inserts in gray perforated suede, accented with sapphire blue welts. This material fared exceptionally well in Ford's 100,000-mile durability test. Door panels sport anniversary cloisonne badges. Senior said he wanted to keep the interior styling subtle in the 35th-Anniversary T-bird. The result is meant to arouse excitement by leaving you hungry for just a little more.

Every car will come with a suede-cleaning kit in a little black box with titanium silver and radiant blue trim. Senior designed that, too. A special plaque will be included with the original owner's name and V.I.N. number of each anniversary model. And each anniversary 'Bird will also arrive with a custom car cover made by the same company that supplies covers to Rolls-Royce.

Unlike some of its competitors, Ford has traditionally kept its limited editions limited, regardless of dealer demand. (The company built only 5,540 20th-Anniversary Cougars, even though it had taken orders for the first 5,000 only 17 days after the car was announced.) Ford plans to build only 5,000 35th-Anniversary Thunderbirds during the 1990 model year. Every one will be a tribute to the company's longest-lived nameplate.

Jerry Senior, the Ford stylist responsible for the 35th-Anniversary T-bird

THUNDERBIRD SALES

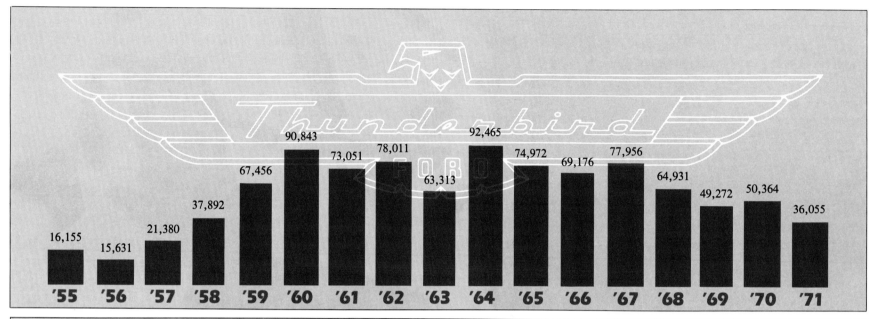

90,843   92,465
73,051   78,011   74,972   77,956
67,456   63,313   69,176   64,931
37,892   49,272   50,364
16,155   15,631   21,380   36,055

'55 '56 '57 '58 '59 '60 '61 '62 '63 '64 '65 '66 '67 '68 '69 '70 '71

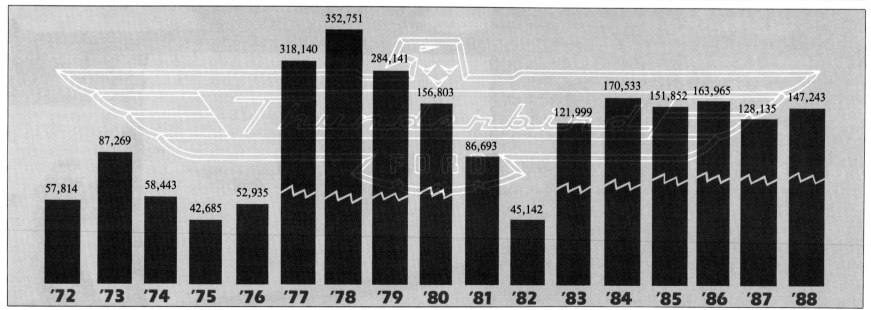

352,751
318,140
284,141
156,803   170,533   151,852   163,965   147,243
121,999   128,135
87,269   86,693
57,814   58,443   52,935   45,142
42,685

'72 '73 '74 '75 '76 '77 '78 '79 '80 '81 '82 '83 '84 '85 '86 '87 '88

NOTE: Broken bar indicates that overall height has been reduced to accommodate space limitations.

BIBLIOGRAPHY

BOOKS

Thunderbird: An Odyssey in Automotive Design, by William P. Boyer (Dallas: Taylor Publishing Company, 1986)

The Thunderbird Story: Personal Luxury, by Richard M. Langworth (Osceola, Wisconsin: Motorbooks International, 1980)

MAGAZINE ARTICLES

Autocar
"Road Test No. 1588: Ford Thunderbird;" February 10, 1956

Automobile Quarterly
"The Short, Happy Flight of the Early Bird," by Karl Ludvigsen; Volume 9, Number 1

"Lincoln Continental 1961-1969: The American Aristocrat," by Dave Emanuel (writing as Nick Cole); Volume 23, Number 4

Car and Driver
"Road Test: Thunderbird Convertible;" August 1964

"Road Test: Ford Thunderbird, Cadillac Eldorado;" November 1966

"Road Test: Ford Thunderbird;" December 1976

"Road Test: Ford Thunderbird" by Rich Ceppes; July 1980

"Road Test: Ford Thunderbird Turbo Coupe" by Larry Griffin; July 1983

"Ford Thunderbird Turbo Coupe: To Soar Like an Eagle" by Rich Ceppes; October 1986

Car Life
"Thunderbird Sports Roadster;" July 1962

"Road Test: Thunderbird 4-Door;" February 1962

"Road Test: Thunderbird — A Home Away From Home;" February 1969

Motor Trend
"Ford Thunderbird" by Walt Woron; December 1954

" '56 Thunderbird and Corvette Road Test" by Walt Woron; June 1956

"Car of the Year!: '58 Thunderbird" by Sam Hanks; May 1958

"Thunderbird: Road Test;" May 1961

"Thunderbird: Road Test" by Jim Wright; September 1962

"Thunderbird: More Fingertip Feathers for the Bird's Plush Nest" by John Ethridge; March 1966

"Almost a Limousine" by Jim Brokaw; December 1970

"1987 Car of the Year: Ford Thunderbird Turbo Coupe;" February 1987

"1989 Car of the Year: Ford Thunderbird SC;" February 1989

Road & Track
"Testing Ford's Personal Car: The T-Bird Shows its Claws;" March 1955

"Flight Testing Ford's Bird;" August 1956

"Road Test: Ford Thunderbird;" June 1959

"Road Test: Ford Thunderbird Turbo Coupe;" January 1983

"Ford Thunderbird Turbo Coupe: The High Price of Progress?" August 1987

Speed Age
"Bob Veith Tests and Compares: Corvette, T-Bird, Golden Hawk" by Bob Veith; May 1957

Sports Cars Illustrated
"Driver's Report: The 1957 Thunderbird" by Karl Ludvigsen; January 1957

"Road Test: Ford's Thunderbird;" April 1958

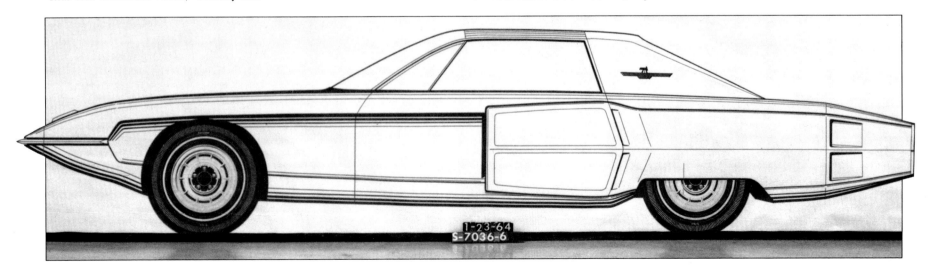

Proposal for the 1967 Thunderbird, drawn in the winter of 1964

INDEX

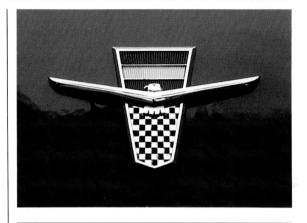

ACKNOWLEDGEMENTS

We are most grateful to the many people at Ford Motor Company who took the time to assist with our research, among them David Caplan, Jerry Cuper, Ted Finney, Gale Halderman, Jim Kennedy, Bruce M. Kopf, Linda Lee, Brad Munn, Charles Ordowski, Allen Ornes, Joel Pitcoff, Mike Richards, Jerry Senior, Dave Turner, and Ken Wagle. Special thanks to Paul M. Preuss, Ford's manager of public affairs, for his tireless efforts on our behalf, and to Ford engineer (and loyal *Automobile Quarterly* subscriber) Paul Castrilli for his generous hospitality.

Thanks also to Don Donahue of the Rocky Mountain 1958-66 Thunderbird Club, Lois Eminger and Marjorie Price of the Classic Thunderbird Club International, Otis Meyer of *Road & Track*, Joseph Oros, and especially Franklin Q. Hershey.

This book is dedicated to my wife, Clorinda, who shares all my adventures.
—JFK

PHOTO CREDITS

Color photography pp. 16, 26-28, 30-32, 34-37, 39, 46-49 by Roy D. Query; pp. 42, 43 top, courtesy Ford Motor Company; pp. 9, 12-15, 19, 22, 43 bottom, 44 top by Rick Lenz; pg. 23 by Vince Manocchi; pg. 44 center, from the *AQ* Archives. All historic advertisments are from the J. Walter Thompson Archive, provided courtesy of the Manuscript Department, William R. Perkins Library, Duke University; except page 12, courtesy Ford Motor Company. All black-and-white photography courtesy Ford Motor Company, except pg. 10 top right, courtesy Franklin Q. Hershey; pg. 11 top, courtesy Classic Thunderbird Club International; pg. 17 lower, from the collection of Greg Sharp.